"Medalling with History"
A History of Vaughtons

Two Centuries of Goldsmithing, Silversmithing, Engravers and Enamellers to the World

Tim Growcott

First published 2015

Text © Tim Growcott

Published by Adrian Baggett, Mapseeker Archive Publishing
Kidlington, Oxford OX5 1DG
Printed by Think Digital Books Ltd in Weston-Super-Mare BS24 7DD

British Library Cataloguing in Publication Data.
A catalogue record for this book is available from the British Library.

ISBN 978-1-84491-838-6 Softcover

Typesetting and design by Adrian Baggett

FOREWORD

My association with Vaughtons began over 30 years ago. I worked then at our family business, C&E Plating with my late father, Mr Ron Hobbis. C&E Plating worked closely with Vaughtons for many years as a supplier for their Gold and Silver electro plating requirements.

It was in 2004 I commenced negotiations to purchase Vaughtons and its associated companies, and in 2005 I was delighted to be in the driving seat!

It became immediately apparent that I had taken on a very unique company, employing highly skilled people. Vaughtons were manufacturing as a tight team, producing a superb product with quality that was second to none.

Vaughtons is a gem of a company, and will hopefully continue to be in my family ownership for many years to come.

Steve Hobbis
Director
WH Darby Ltd

CONTENTS

INTRODUCTION

As with most histories, this volume came about in a completely different conversation.

W H Darby's management team were in due process of tendering for the 2012 Olympic medal (they had previously produced the 1908 version) and on further investigation, whilst there appeared to be "War and Peace" on other Birmingham and London based medallists and coin makers, Vaughtons was almost anonymously absent; it was though the company had never existed other than in trade catalogues and some limited archive material. Even searches on the world wide web showed almost a complete dearth of source material. There was no history of the company... so we thought we would write it accordingly.

Ever one for the challenge we have pieced together this history rather akin to doing the jigsaw without "the picture on the box"; pieces were there but no one knew quite how or where they all fitted together.

What we did find was what a phenomenal company Vaughton was, existing for almost 200 years, Birmingham based, with a global reputation for high quality gold-smithing, silver-smithing, enamelling, engraving, carving, plating, polishing and all manner of masonic, military, colonial and commonwealth regalia, medals, coins, badges, spoons, gifts and localosities even the repair and refurbishment of judges wigs. A treasure trove of armorial, civic, heraldic, Olympic, sporting memorabilia commemorating heroic and tragic circumstances. From the FA cup to Titanic, from Neville Chamberlain, MP and PM, to Oliver Vaughton, England, Aston Villa and FA Cup hero... all remembered and celebrated in Birmingham's craftsmanship and skills.

From its inception in 1819 to the present day the Vaughton brand has maintained its continuing existence to the present day activities undertaken at W H Darby's premises in Well Street, Birmingham.

I have tried to establish more of the family and company history from origins to today but one cannot fail to be drawn to the sheer diversity and standards of works undertaken. It's a common saying "You can always tell a Brummie, but you can't tell him much!!!!"

From simple beginnings Vaughtons became the largest medallist and regalia company in the UK... not bad for a Brummie.

Tim Growcott

CHAPTER ONE – EARLY DAYS

Through premises at Little Hampton Street, Hampton Street, Great Hampton Row, Great Hampton Street, Constitution Hill, Vyse Street, Hockley Street, Livery Street and finally Well Street the Vaughton story exemplifies the successes and failures of a once prolific and highly localised industry. Many similar companies succumbed to the Jewellery Quarters demise in the 1980's.

The Vaughton brand continues towards its bi–centenary. How many more kings, queens, princes, princesses, lords, ladies, shahs, emperors, ambassadors, mayors, masters, majors, admirals, generals and other captains of industry amongst others will be recipients of its activities?

The Jewellery Quarter

The Jewellery Quarter is an area situated in the south of the Hockley Area of Birmingham. It officially encompasses approximately 0.41 square miles (1.07 square kilometres). Its existence is universally synonymous with the manufacture of jewellery but also and more significantly in this case for the manufacture of coins and medals. It was here that the "Vaughton's" story flowered, blossomed and is still maintained today.

Circa 1610 Birmingham was a relatively small environ, much smaller than Coventry or Warwick; this being established by reference to the John Speede map of that year.

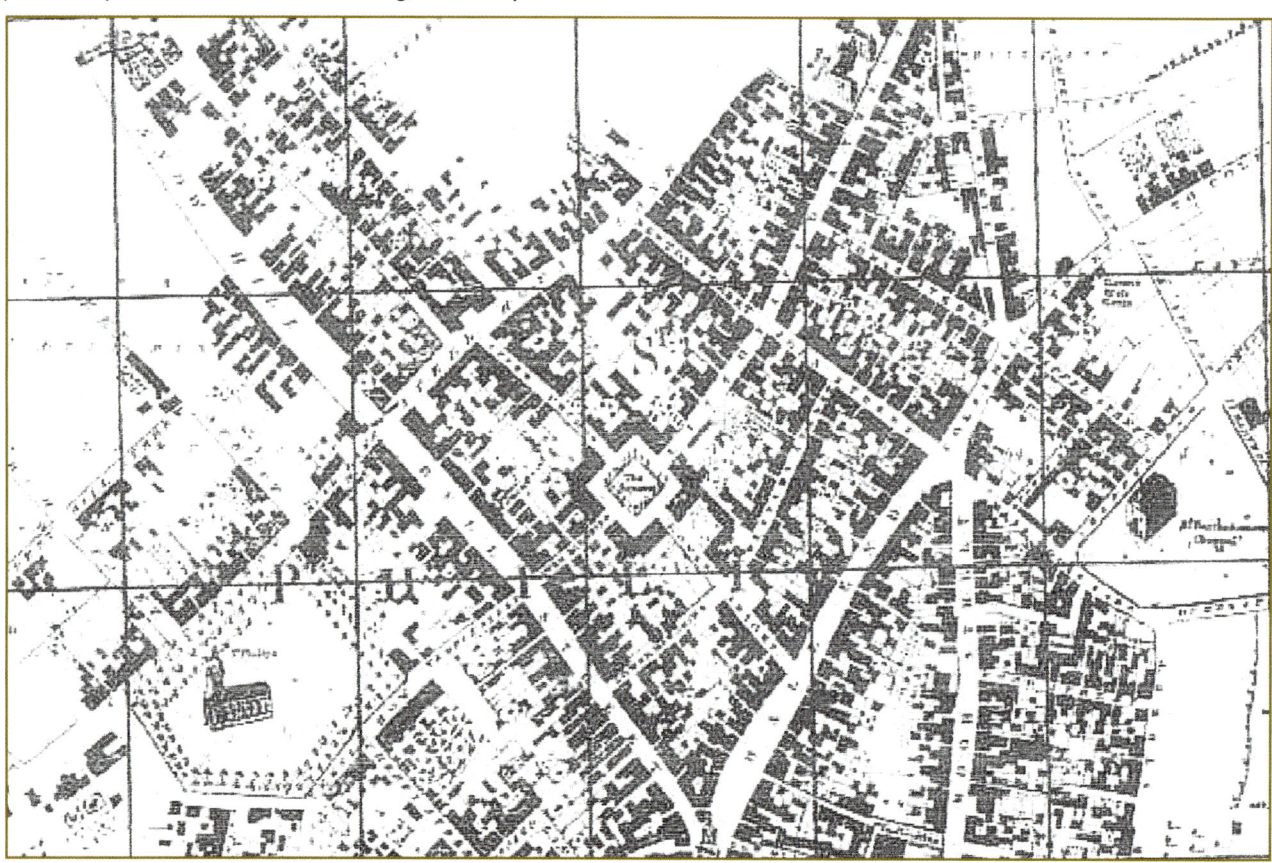

The 1750 Birmingham map, surveyed by S Bradford, shows Livery Street in its infancy.

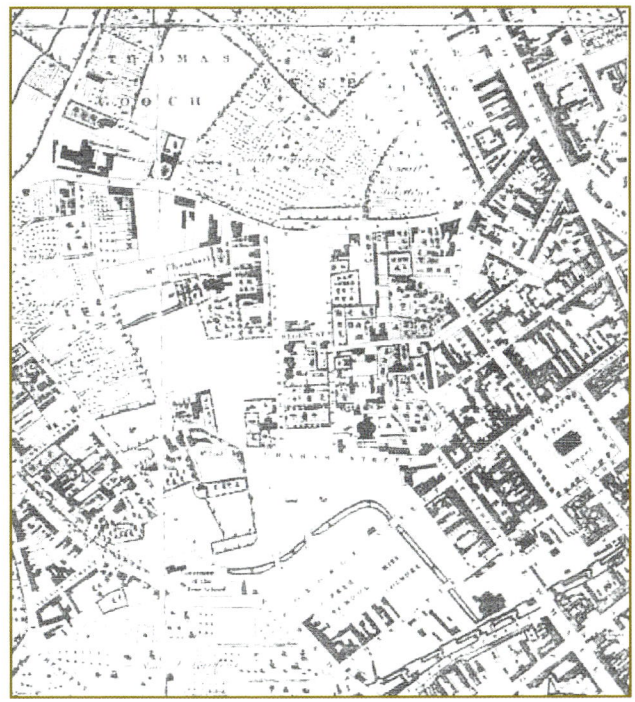

The Pigott map of Birmingham 1828 (as surveyed in 1824) shows how rapidly the Quarter developed and whilst the future location of Well Street is shown as open fields, off Great Hampton Street, the 135 Constitution Hill site and Livery Street locations are duly indicated. The following map shows parts of Gooch Street and Vyse Estates where the Jewellery Quarter was located and St Paul's and St George's parishes established.

Roger Pemberton was named in a 1553 survey as one of Birmingham's first goldsmiths.

Birmingham Assay Office was established in 1773.

During the 18th and 19th centuries a considerable trade developed in the manufacture of medals, coins, buttons, cap badges and pins in addition to small metal toys. Birmingham became the "Workshop of the World" and Vaughtons a significant player in the city's business

By the mid 1800's the area was considered as one of the most lucrative in the city with some of the best paid workers. There were also more people employed in the trade than in any other UK city. Boys were given apprenticeships at 14 and on average earned four shillings (20 pence). This would increase until they were 21 after which they then obtained full employment.

By 1861 approximately 7,500 people worked in the area's jewellery trade and in 1880 there were almost 700 listed workshops. The area further developed due to the declining price of gold and from the technological developments of new processes such as electroplating, which was developed by George Elkington at the Elkington Silver Electroplating Works in Newhall Street.

By 1883 less than half of Birmingham's jewellery trade silver was of sufficient standard to pass through the Assay Office however no less than 32.363 tonnes of silvery jewellery and 3.4093 tonnes of gold items were received via over 2. 6 million articles sent for assaying.

The British Jewellers' and Silversmiths' Association was founded in 1887, and in 1890 a School of Jewellery and Silversmithing was established in a converted factory on Vittoria Street as a branch of the School of Art.

The area's industry reached its peak in 1914 with in excess of 20,000 personnel being employed. Sadly the Quarter was hit hard by the Great Depression and a steady decline started.

Following the 2nd World War the Quarter witnessed a brief recovery but by 1948 larger manufacturing entities were in decline. The industry has continued to decline throughout the post war years, mainly due to a lack of demand and the adverse impact of overseas competition.

In 1965 approximately 8,000 people were employed in 900 businesses but by 1985 this was down to approximately 4,000 in 600 businesses.

In 1987 the Quarter again began to change as a warehouse in St Paul's Square was converted to flats. Anvic House was refurbished into workshops; by 1998 over 25% of the Quarter's industrial establishments were vacant and only 3% of the area was occupied by families.

In addition to Vaughtons many other businesses plied their trade within the Birmingham area and included Thomas Fattorini, J R Gaunt, Millers, W O Lewis, W Reeves, Toye Kenning and Spencer, L Simpson, Marples & Beasley, B H Collins, W J Dingley, J Pinches, F Cobb, Gladman and Norman and many others including Birmingham Medal, Miller and Thomas, Fattorini used their own marks as did Vaughtons, but as many as half of all work produced never had marking done. Vaughtons' marks are referred to latter on.

Many of these companies were deemed to be to product specific and failed as a consequence of this. Vaughtons however had such an extensive product diversity and standard of workmanship that despite adversity continue till today.

The presence of "Vaughtons" in the Jewellery Quarter and its locale are summarised below; this being sourced from miscellaneous directories.

Year	Name	Occupation	Address
1781	Vaughton, Philip	Toymaker	32 St. John's Street
1835	Vaughton & Bailey	Gold Seal and Key Maker	6 Little Hampton Street
1839	Vaughton P	Gold Seal and Key Maker	6 Little Hampton Street
1845	Vaughton Philip	Working Jeweller	127 Hampton Street
1849	Vaughton Philip	Working Jeweller	127 Hampton Street
1855	Vaughton Philip & Son	Working Jeweller	127 Hampton Street
1862	Vaughton Philip	Working Jeweller	127 Hampton Street
1866	Vaughton P & Sons	Jewellers	127 Hampton Street
1866	Vaughton Philip	Manufacturing Jeweller	50 Hockley Street
1872	Vaughton Philip & Sons	Goldsmiths & Jewellers	1 Great Hampton Street
1872	Vaughton Philip	Jeweller	21 Vyse Street
1873	Vaughton P & Sons	Goldsmith & Jewellery Manufacturers	1a Great Hampton Street
1876	Vaughton Phillip & Sons	Goldsmith & Jeweller	1 Great Hampton Street
1880	Vaughton Phillip & Sons	Goldsmith & Jeweller	1 Great Hampton Street
1883	Vaughton P & Sons	Goldsmith and Jewellers	193 Great Hampton Row
1883	Vaughton, Edward	Jeweller	4 Warstone Lane
1883	Vaughton, Oliver	Jeweller	193 Great Hampton Row
1883	Vaughton, Philip	Jeweller	21 Vyse Street
1884	Vaughton P & Sons	Jeweller	193 Great Hampton Row
1892	Vaughton	Medals and Badges	Gothic Works
1892	Vaughton P & Sons	Manufacturing Jewellers	193 Great Hampton Row
1892	Vaughton Bros	Die Sinkers	133 ½ Constitution Hill
1896	Vaughton P & Sons also Thomas Albert Vaughton	Manufacturing Jeweller	193 Great Hampton Row

Goldsmithing, Silversmithing and medals were not the only ideas that came from "Vaughtons"; an abstract from "Early Cycle Lighting" by Peter W Card shows that; -

Taken from book,

Early Cycle Lighting
by Peter W Card
published by
Crowwood Publishing

"Harry Lucas had a friend a Mr Vaughton a Jeweller and Medalist, who came up with an idea for an improved accumulator cell for cycle lighting, Lucas manufactured it, but due to cost, the idea did not take off.

Mr Lucas and Mr Vaughton where both cyclist's that being how they met".

"Harry Lucas had a friend, a Mr Vaughton, a jeweller and medallist, who came up with an idea for an improved accumulator cell for cycle lighting. Lucas manufactured it, but due to cost, the idea did not take off"

"Mr Lucas and Mr Vaughton were both cyclists, that being how they met"

Harry Lucas was of course the driving force of Lucas of electrical systems fame. Lucas became a major player in the automotive industry.

At a time when medallists included Allen & Moore, Jenkins, Fenwick, Ottley, Pinches, Restall, Sale, Spink and Wyon, Vaughtons grew to be the largest of them all.

The following page shows the Vaughtons Company's Memorandum of Association, still on display at the Well Street premises of W H Darby.

THE COMPANIES (CONSOLIDATION) ACT, 1908.

COMPANY LIMITED BY SHARES.

Memorandum of Association

OF

VAUGHTONS LIMITED.

1. The name of the Company is VAUGHTONS LIMITED.

2. The Registered Office of the Company will be situate in England.

3. The objects for which the Company is established are as follows :—

> (a) To purchase and acquire, take over, carry on, and develop, as from the 31st day of December 1908, the business of a Silversmith, Goldsmith and General Manufacturer, formerly carried on by Thomas Albert Vaughton under the style of " Philip Vaughton and Sons," and the business of Diesinkers and Stampers, carried on by the said Thomas Albert Vaughton, Oliver Howard Vaughton, and Philip Henry Vaughton, in Livery Street Birmingham, under the style of " Vaughton Brothers," together with any property and assets as set out in the Agreements hereafter mentioned, belonging to them in connection with the said businesses, and to undertake all the liabilites in connection with the said businesses, and with a view thereto to enter into and carry into effect, (with or without modification) an agreement already prepared and engrossed, and expressed to be made between the

CHAPTER TWO –
VAUGHTON FAMILY HISTORY

Tracing Vaughton lineage takes us back to a Philip Vaughton (DOB unknown), he had 3 recorded sons, Philip, (baptised 27.05.1743), John (baptised 01.7.1748) and Luke (baptised 30.11.1745, died 1842). (A "Philip Vaughton" is noted in a 1781 miscellaneous trade reference as working as a "Toy maker at 32 John Street").

The "Founding Father" of the Vaughton company (est. 1819) was Philip Vaughton, born in 1769. He was the son of John Vaughton (baptised 1748) and Elizabeth. The Vaughton lineage is traversed by large families across the generations. "Philip", "Luke" and "John" became recurrent and enduring names for the male line and 4 such Philips exist within the first 4 generations.

Philip Vaughton, founding father (b. 1769), had two sons after marrying Mary Hares (or Ayres), Philip (born 1802, died 1863) and Luke (born 1801, died 1849). This Philip (b. 1802) then produced at least 5 recorded children, 3 boys and 2 girls; Thomas (b. 1831), Elizabeth (b. 1832), Mary Ann (b. 1835), Oliver (b. 1839) and Charles (b. 1840).

Luke (b. 1801) produced at least 9 recorded children, 3 boys and 6 girls, Mary (b. 1821), Maria (b. 1826), Philip (b. 1826), Elizabeth (b. 1826), Sarah (b. 1828), Luke (b. 1828), Edward (b. 1832), Emma (b. 1837) and Louisa (b. 1839). This generation's Philip's wife is recorded as Mary. Strangely Luke also married a Mary (her recorded d.o.b 1796).

Again trade references (1835) refer to Vaughton & Bayley and (1839) as P Vaughton as "Gold Seal and Key makers" working out of businesses at 6 Little Hampton Street, Birmingham". From trade references of the period (1845–1866), the business is based at 127 Hampton Street, Birmingham, all indicating "Working Jewellers".

In concentrating on the male lineage, Philip's 3 sons then produced at least 8 sons, whilst Luke's five sons produced a further seven male issue.

Philip's son Thomas (b. 1831) married Rosina in 1831, then producing Thomas Albert (b. 1860), Oliver Howard (b. 1861 d.1937), Ernest E (b.

1863), Florence A (b. 1865), Philip H (b. 1867), Rosina J (b. 1869), Sidney H (b. 1870), Arthur K (b. 1871), Walter S (b. 1873), Gertrude A (b. 1875) and Frederick W (b. 1877).

Oliver Howard Vaughton married and had six children one boy and 5 girls, Howard George (b. 1989 d. 1970), Annie, Catherine, Aileen, Doris and Grace.

This generation included Oliver Howard Vaughton who became an Aston Villa and England Football player, winning the FA Cup in 1887 and yet another Philip to continue the family name and jewellery business and the famous architect Sidney H Vaughton who was responsible for the execution of the Vaughton's "Gothic Works" in Livery Street.

In a similar vein, Luke (b. 1801 d1848), his son Philip (b. 1826) married one Eliza Cotteril (b. 1827). His son Thomas (b. 1831) married Rosina and produced Thomas Albert (b. 1860). His son Luke (b. 1828) married Selina and produced Kate (b. 1853), Clara (b. 1857), Susan (b. 1859), Luke (b. 1861), Frederick (b. 1864), Betty (b. 1866), Lizzie (b. 1868) and Thomas (b. 18710.

Luke (b. 1801), his son Edward married and produced Edward E (b. 1857), Amelia E (b. 1859), Philip Gilbert (b. 1861), Vincent V (b. 1864), Leonard H (b. 1865) and Ada Gertrude (b. 1868).

Howard George (b. 1898) married and his two sons, Brian and John are the last in the direct Vaughton lineage directly involved with the company.

P Vaughton was officially formed as a company in 1819, but Philip (b. 1775) was working under the family name as early as 1811. From this inception the family tree was rapidly expanding and within this developed P Vaughton, P Vaughton and Son (working at 193 Great Hampton Row and 92 Livery Street), P Vaughton and Sons, Vaughtons (working at Great Hampton Place) and John Vaughton (working at 21 Vyse Street).

All names note in blue are formally recorded as jewellers, goldsmiths and or silversmiths. Census records also show that a number of the family were employed as Japaners and Clerks.

In researching this genealogy what was self-evident was the considerable number of infant deaths within the early generations. As such, we have been unable to define all members of the family.

Census records show that Philip Vaughton (b. 1802) resided at 127 Hampton Street (1851 census), 87 Lozells Road (1861 and 71 census) and 118 Heathfield Road (1881 census).

Philip (b. 1826) is recorded at 21 Vyse Street (1861 and 1871 census).

Thomas (b. 1831) is recorded at 127 Hampton Road (1861 census, 129 Trinity Road (1881 census) and finally 94 Trinity Road (1891 census).

Luke (b. 1828) is recorded at 123 Well Street (1861 and 1871 census) and 25 James Street (1881 census).

Edward (b. 1832) is recorded as residing at 195 Warstones Lane (1861 census), 47 Augusta Street (1871 census), 15 Claremont Road, Handsworth (1881 census) and 32 Claremont Road, Handsworth (1891 census).

Oliver (b. 1839) is recorded as residing at 118 Heathfield Road, with his mother and Mary Ann(1891 census).

George Brian Vaughton now resides in Exminster, and his brother John Howard in Monmouth.

The following family trees show this in a more graphic manner.

The last Vaughton with a controlling interest in the business was Brian, who transferred the controlling interest to Pat Taylor in 1966. From there the Company was taken over by W H Darby in 1997.

Family interests continue and I am indebted to John and Brian Vaughton who continue to maintain the interest in their family and its business history.

(Please see Appendix 1 & 2)

CHAPTER THREE – VAUGHTON PREMISES

Vaughtons has over its history occupied several premises, the first probably being recorded as 6 Little Hampton Street (1835). The 1845 Directory records Vaughton and Bailey at 127 Hampton Street, Birmingham. 50 Hockley Street then enters the Directory record.

The following relates information on the more modern Vaughton premises.

135 Constitution Hill

Birmingham was once the centre of the world's button making industry with records showing manufacture as early as 1166. In 1700 there were 104 recorded button manufacturers within the city bounds. Firmin, Gaunt, Jennens, Armfield and Pitt were the major players at the turn of the 19th Century.

In 1897 the firm was known as Vaughton Brothers, located at 135 Constitution Hill, Birmingham. References list the company as "Buttonmakers, Medallists and Mints".

The ubiquitous brass button was a mainstay of Birmingham enterprise from the late Victorian to 1930's and they were produced in their millions for an unlimited range of use; military, naval and civic uniforms, railway livery, club and society, colleges, hunts, shipping lines, sporting clubs, corporation, transport and tramway. Trouser buttons were often produced as a single worked piece, mainly in brass. Many companies, including Vaughton Bros, impressed their makers name. (This was also true of Vaughtons Gothic Works produced items). These brass buttons were relatively easy to produce having simple sourcing from low cost dies.

It was from here that Vaughtons moved to their Livery Street "Gothic Works"

The last vestige of prior Vaughton occupancy is defined by the building's letter box.

1 Great Hampton Street

Vaughton's continuance at 1 Great Hampton Street is only recorded on a single surviving advertising flier and the Birmingham Directories of the period. The move took place between 1866 and 1872 as the business continued to expand.

The building no longer exists having been demolished for the building of the Lucas Factory. The Lucas factory was a landmark for the locality in that it replaced the traditional brick built format by the use of a steel skeleton in the same theme as American skyscrapers were being built. There are many photographs of the Lucas plant being constructed such was its innovative method of construction

The coincidence is that clearly there was a link between Mr Vaughton and Mr Lucas which initiated Mr Vaughton's bicycle oriented accumulator equipment. Whilst this ultimately was unsuccessful it demonstrates that Vaughtons were always open to new markets and opportunities.

Sadly no building plans exist and photographs have been too poor to reproduce.

Vaughtons became increasingly innovative in their goods and the automotive sector, and Lucas became a significant supplier to all of the UK Motor Trade. Vaughtons would go on to supply vehicle badges of all manner to support Birmingham's motor industry.

193 Great Hampton Row

Vaughtons next move was to premises at 193 Great Hampton Row, again dates are open but from Birmingham directories this took place over the period between 1880 and 1884.

The building was demolished to make way for modern flats in the Birmingham expansion and the move to bring in local housing.

4 Warstone Lane

In 1883 4 Warstone Lane was recorded as the premises of Edward Vaughton, Jeweller.

The premises is currently occupied by "Lloyds Jewellery Workshop".

21 Vyse Street

In 1872 21 Vyse Street is recorded as the premises of Philip Vaughton, Jeweller. The property is currently occupied by "Fellows Antiques and Gold".

16 Well Street

The current home of the "Vaughtons" brand lies within the W H Darby premises in Well Street, Birmingham. W H Darby is a family owned business, itself established in 1886, with a continuing passion for fine crafted regalia. The building was first occupied in 1960 and its two floors house offices, display area, Press Shop, Plating Shop, workshops, Goods Inwards and Outwards, but still using the same basic skills that would have been developed through Great Hampton Row, Great Hampton Street and Livery Street.

The Vaughtons brand still reflects the highest standards of craftsmanship and quality with one aim, supplying superb products. As with Vaughtons, W H Darby was founded by a "Brummie", working as a die sinker in the Jewellery Quarter.

The company has partnerships with T J Skelton, established 1885 and C E Plating, established 1951. These partners are all associated with the traditions first established over 20 years ago.

C E Plating specialise in gold and silver plating and their skills are used to produce superior quality products. The plating ranges include 18 and 24-carat hard gold, black gold, rose gold, dull and bright copper, bronze and tin, dull nickel, rhodium, silver and antique silver and chrome finishing.

92–95 Livery Street.

In 1903 the company moved to premises at 92–95 Livery Street, Birmingham. This is the most spectacular of all Vaughton premises.

Under the heading 'Vaughton Gothic Works' there is mention of the new building in a Birmingham Civic Society newsletter; *"To this day it is an impressive building, and noted in particular were 'its excellent terracotta details, especially the lettering'"*. It was here that Vaughtons medal and badge production continued.

The company maintained its specialised work in regard to mayoral chains and civic regalia and jewellery, spoons, cups and trophies, nameplates and coins and badges.

Referring to the Memorandum of Association in 1908; *"'the business of a Silversmith, Goldsmith and General Manufacturer' was formerly carried on by Thomas Albert Vaughton under the style of "Philip Vaughton and Sons""*.

An abstract from the 1906 Vaughton catalogue reads;

We beg to announce we are at all times prepared to submit designs and estimates for all kinds of Civic and Armorial Work in Gold, Silver, Bronze, Silver–Plate and Steel.

Our Manufactory and Plant have been completely modernised, so that we are now able to supply our friends with Goods of the highest quality and lowest possible price: but while bringing our methods of manufacture up-to-date, we have not neglected the Artistic and handicraft side of the business. Goldsmithing and Silversmithing, together with such processes as Embossing, Engraving, carving, Chiselling, Inlaying, Enamelling, etc., must always remain handicrafts in the true sense of the word, and it will now be found that our craftsmen in these branches are second to none in the country.

Special attention is paid to the carrying out of Antique and Heraldic designs, and the greatest care is taken to preserve distinctive character.

We undertake Heraldic Architectural and Antiquarian Research in connection with or arising out of work entrusted to us.

A lithograph of the building is shown, abstracted from the Vaughton 1906 catalogue.

It shows the building as it stood with open ground found to the Snow Hill side and the "Crocodile Works" to its rear.

The "Crocodile Works" was a producer of bayonets. Today the building produces stampings, including parts for Jaguar Cars.

The 2nd FA Cup was produced here and a plaque located by the main entrance still records this.

The main entrance also has photographs of one of the most famous "Vaughtons", Howard Vaughton, the founder's grandson, played for Aston Villa and England, scored the winning goal in an FA Cup final, and was also a renowned speed skater, tennis player and cricketer. He also established the silversmithing side of the business and went on to become a Director of Aston Villa.

The building reflected the success of Vaughtons and its architect, Sidney H Vaughton, constructed it in 1902 in the "free Jacobean" style. The style encompassed steeply pitched roof elements, prominent cross gables, tall narrow windows, prominent chimneys and elegant open design elements.

The slate roofed building was titled "Vaughton's Gothic Works" and its exterior was adorned with terra cotta dressings over red brick work, also detailing "Goldsmiths" and "Silversmiths", these were later chiselled off in the late 1970's as they crumbled and fell in part to the pavement below.

The building is currently listed as a Grade II structure. Livery Street's name is derived from Swann's Riding Academy that was once located there. The current building occupier is the Hatters Hostel and many features of the original building have been retained. Whilst Gothic Works was operational it housed the management offices at the front of the building, plus an extensive showroom. Outside this room, with its steel security gate, there was a large oval display unit housing an impressive selection of some of the medals and badges produced by the firm. This display may now be in the hands of the Birmingham City Museum.

The company was sold and, according to the Birmingham Civic Society, remained at Gothic Works until 1997, when fellow trophy manufacturer W H Darby acquired the firm and transferred it to premises at 16 Well Street in Hockley. Sadly, although Vaughtons still operates today, no member of the family now owns a share in the company.

The original doors, stairs, entrance floor, windows and general fitting remain as original although the basement floors remained waterlogged up till 18 months ago.

The building now stands in a much changed Livery Street, with modern apartments and buildings directly adjacent to the Jewellery Quarter side however the old Joseph Cook & Sons building with its equally impressive frontage remains on the Snow Hill side.

The factory was built to replace the earlier works at 135 Constitution Hill and comprised two separate buildings, one of which fronts onto Livery Street, the other a free standing workshop located behind a small open backyard.

The front block had a typical "of the time" T-plan: the T - cross being formed by a street range of two stories with a façade executed in red brick and terra cotta. The T–stem was formed by a two storey workshop built of both red and "blue" bricks. The building to the rear has a two storey

range adjoined by a larger single story block with a north lit ridge and furrow roof, this later arrangement again being typical of construction at the turn of the century.

The form of the works was very much of an early Jewellery Quarter manufactory, with T plan and wide workshop range occupying the centre of the plot. This arrangement usually left a limited amount of space for narrow flanking yards.

The building's original plans are retained within Birmingham museum's archives but little else remains other than the 1906, 1915, 1922, 1937 and 1954 catalogues and some miscellaneous trade pamphlets (Birmingham Museum Archives and Heritage references L62.65 and MS 2369/1/2).

There do however remain employees who worked at Livery Street and can recall with implicit detail the works areas and personnel and there are still former Vaughton employees working at W H Darby at their Well Street premises, continuing the prized "Vaughton" brand tradition.

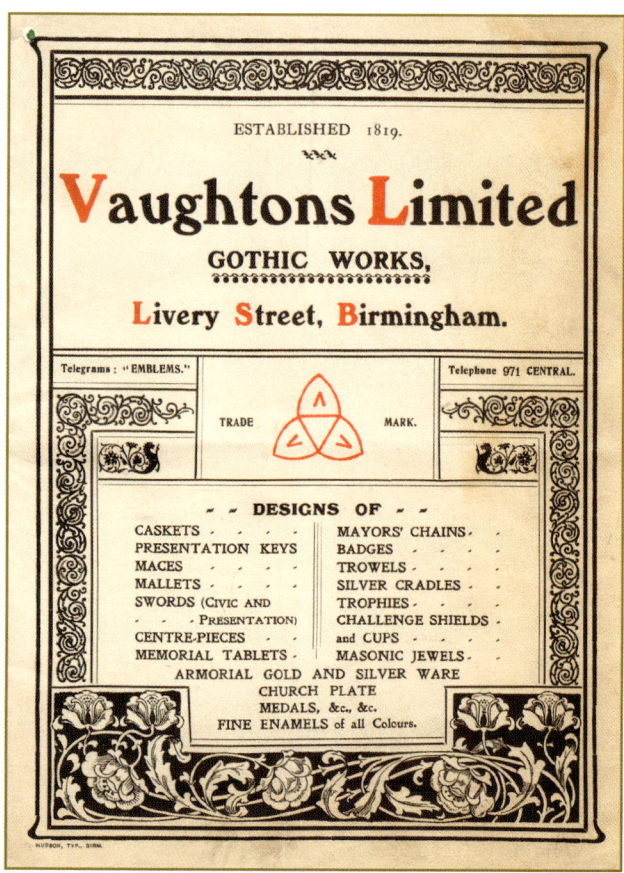

CHAPTER FOUR –
VAUGHTONS GOODS AND SERVICES

The Vaughton brand has always been associated with high quality workmanship in goldsmithing, silversmithing, enamelling, carving, chiselling, inlaying, anodising, electroplating, polishing, embossing, engraving and all other associated press and die work. In detailing what has been produced in almost 200 years of continuous manufacturing it would be easier to state what hasn't been made at their various premises.

Most of the items being produced were available in gold, silver, bronze, brass, silverplate and steel and many of the surviving catalogues show goods with pricing reflecting the medal or items in each of the available materials. The early years of Vaughtons was very much allied to the handicraft, aesthetic and artistic aspects of production, with automation only being more relevant after the early 1900's where mass production of goods dictated the need for high volume supply of consistent and highly reproducible standards. This being dictated by low cost: high volume considerations.

Vaughton's established early on a reputation for superb medals and enamelling and were invariably aligned to well designed and detailed die work and indeed made some of the finest pieces available throughout their history. The sheer intricacy of the craftsman's toil is as evident today as it was almost 200 years ago, and whilst the employees have come and gone, their tools are still readily recognisable today and in constant use.

Whilst medals, civic, military and commemorative and badges have been the backbone of business the following items have all found their way into the company's workbenches.

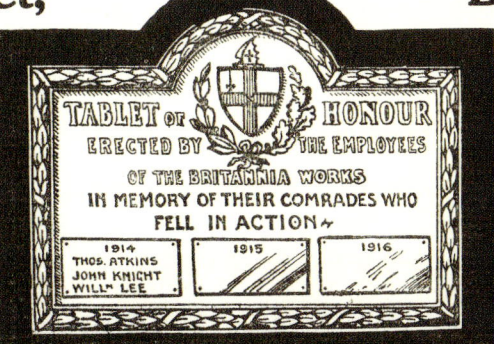

Awarded **GRAND PRIX** { IMPERIAL INTERNATIONAL EXHIBITION, 1909.
JAPAN-BRITISH EXHIBITION, 1910.
FESTIVAL OF EMPIRE EXHIBITION, 1911.

VAUGHTONS Ltd.,

Gothic Works,

Livery Street,   **Birmingham.**

TABLET OF HONOUR
ERECTED BY THE EMPLOYEES
OF THE BRITANNIA WORKS
IN MEMORY OF THEIR COMRADES WHO
FELL IN ACTION

| 1914 THOS. ATKINS JOHN KNIGHT WILLM LEE | 1915 | 1916 |

Memorial Tablets.   **Scrolls of Honour.**

Contractors to the Admiralty, War Office, Post Office, Royal Mint and various Colonial and Foreign Governments.

TERMS : Customers ordering for the first time will oblige by sending cash or reference with order.
Goods sent on approbation on receipt of satisfactory reference or deposit of half value.

Armorial and Civic Regalia including chains of office, additional bars, badges and medals of office

Awards and Gifts

Buttons, Army, Admiralty and Royal Air Force military service uniform and non–military uses

Bicycle Lighting Accumulator Cells (Lucas)

Brooches

Cases and caskets

Colonial and Commonwealth ephemera

Watches, Pins, Lockets and Chains

Coins

Trophies, Teapots, Table Cruet Sets and Cutlery

Cups, including 2 of the 5 FA Cups; the company created the finely crafted 1896 cup as a replacement for the original, stolen from a local shop whilst in the care of the winning Aston Villa team. The 4 kilogram trophy cost just £25 to make originally but was sold recently to David Gold, the owner then of Birmingham City FC, for the amazing price of £480,000.

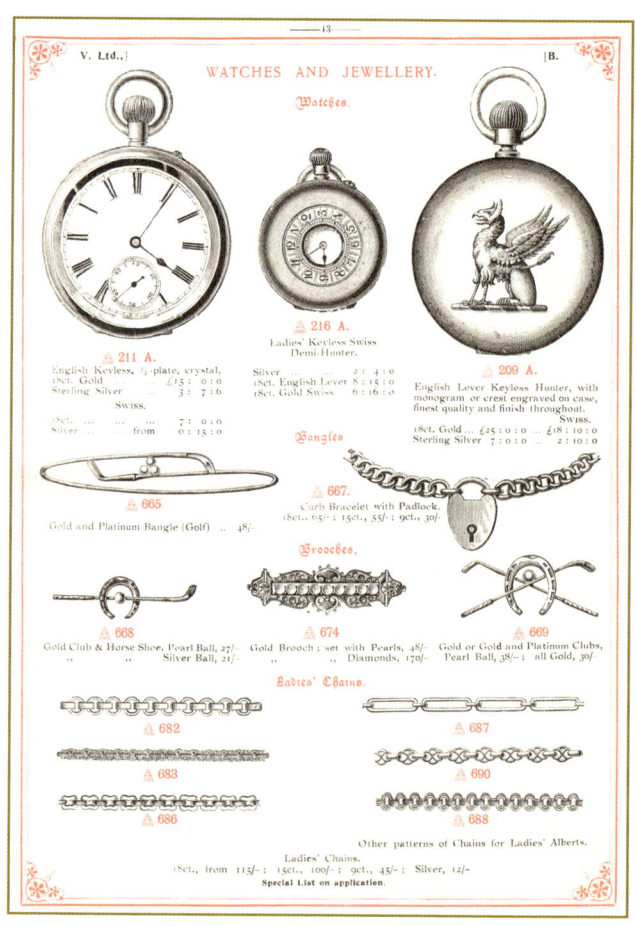

7209 S
Wreath and Shield. Stock reverse in various sizes.

2in. Silver	... 14/-	Bronze	... 5/-
1¾in. ,,	... 10/5	,,	... 3/6
1½in. ,,	... 7/6	,,	... 2/9

211
" SCIENCE," by Albert Toft.
1¾in. diam.
Silver ... 10/6   Bronze ... 3/6
Also made in other sizes.

4001 X
Cup.

Height.	Silver.		E.P.
5½in.	£2 0 0	...	£1 0 0
7in.	3 0 0	...	1 10 0
8in.	4 10 0	...	2 2 0
10in.	6 0 0	...	3 0 0

A24
Military Medal.

9ct. Gold...	... 68/-
Silver	... 8/3
Bronze	... 3/-

Special Die extra.

VI.
Coronation Medal.
(Modelled by Frank Bowcher.)
Samples and prices on application.

264
Committee Badges.
Any other officer's title may be substituted
Enamelled.

		Best Plate.		Silver H.M.
1 doz.	...	1/3	...	3/- each.
3 ,,	...	1/-	...	2/6 ,,

AO 1
Saw-pierced and Engraved Ribbon, Gold Wreath.

9ct. Gold	...	... 28/6
All Silver	...	... 5/6
Bronze	...	... 2/9

VS6

9ct. Gold 30/-	...
Silver 4/6	...
Bronze 2/-	...

VS8

32/-	...
5/-	...
2/6	...

VS7

28/-
4/6
2/-

180b
School Badge.
(Cost of Die, 55/-)

Silver	...	... 12/- doz.
Best Plate	...	... 5/6 ,,

Cuff Links

Commemorative Plaques

Commemorative Spoons and Knives

Court Wigs (Judicial) and Localosities Fobs

Football League Medals (since 1911) including the FA cup winners and losers' medals and the recent Carling Cup (Aston Villa vs Manchester United) medals.

Fraternal Society Regalia including chains of office and medals of office. Heraldic Regalia including chains, shields, mace, rods and associated pieces.

Masonic Regalia including all Craft, Provincial and Grand Lodge jewels, working tools, gavels, glove, sash and apron decorations, column and wand adornments, centre pieces as well as all manner of localosities (these being specific items made at the request of the lodge).

Nameplates of all manner, including those installed on

RMS Titanic and Neville Chamberlain's coffin.

Ribbons.

Shields, sporting, armorial, mayoral and heraldic. The company still has in its archives armorial and heraldic reference texts and volumes with missing pages where a city's crest has been cut out to use as the template for a work piece.

Sporting medals including the 1908 Olympic Medals.

Tankards.

Tie Pins

Velvet Collars.

Whistles.

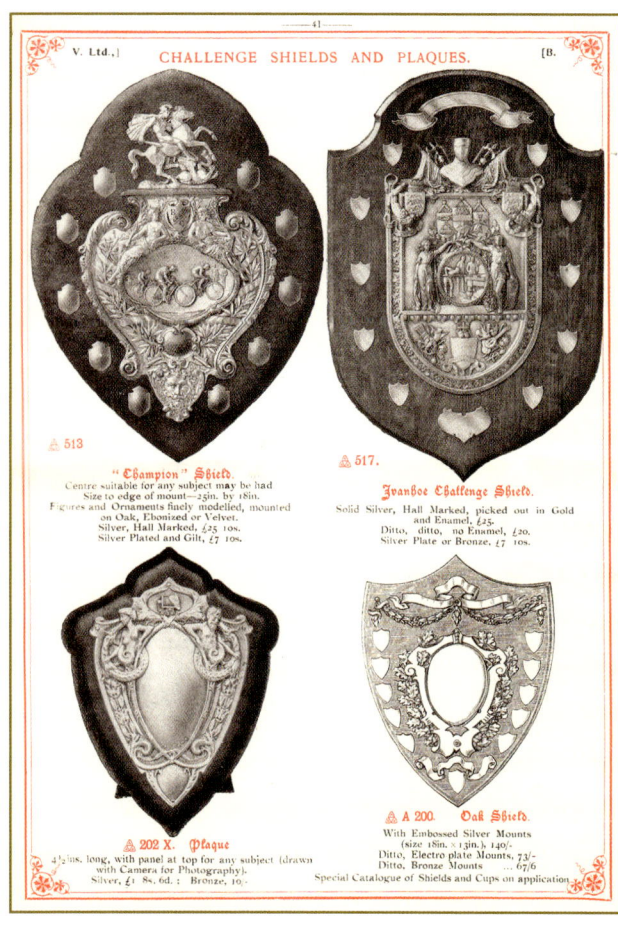

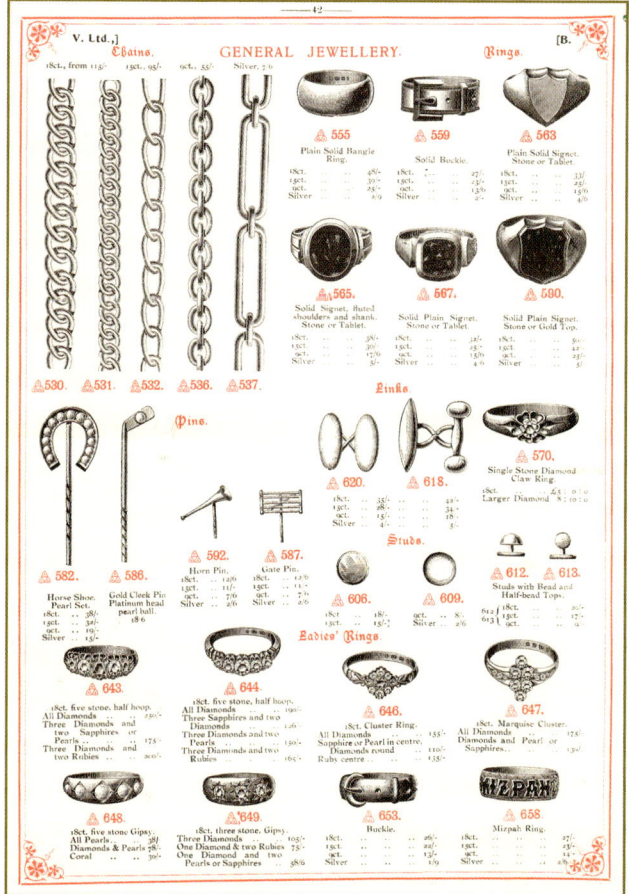

—41—

V. Ltd.,] CHALLENGE SHIELDS AND PLAQUES. [B.

513

"Champion" Shield.

Centre suitable for any subject may be had
Size to edge of mount—25in. by 18in.
Figures and Ornaments finely modelled, mounted on Oak, Ebonized or Velvet.
Silver, Hall Marked, £25 10s.
Silver Plated and Gilt, £7 10s.

517.

Ivanhoe Challenge Shield.

Solid Silver, Hall Marked, picked out in Gold and Enamel, £25.
Ditto, ditto, no Enamel, £20.
Silver Plate or Bronze, £7 10s.

202 X. **Plaque**

4½ins. long, with panel at top for any subject (drawn with Camera for Photography).
Silver, £1 8s. 6d. ; Bronze, 10/-

A 200. **Oak Shield.**

With Embossed Silver Mounts (size 18in. × 13in.), 140/-
Ditto, Electro plate Mounts, 73/-
Ditto, Bronze Mounts ... 67/6

Special Catalogue of Shields and Cups on application.

—42—

V. Ltd.,] GENERAL JEWELLERY. [B.

Chains.

18ct., from 115/- 15ct., 95/- 9ct., 55/- Silver, 7/6

530. 531. 532. 536. 537.

Rings.

555 Plain Solid Bangle Ring.
18ct. 48/-
15ct. 39/-
9ct. 25/-
Silver 2/9

559 Solid Buckle.
18ct. 27/-
15ct. 23/-
9ct. 13/6
Silver 2/-

563 Plain Solid Signet. Stone or Tablet.
18ct. 33/-
15ct. 25/-
9ct. 15/6
Silver 4/6

565. Solid Signet, fluted shoulders and shank. Stone or Tablet.
18ct. 38/-
15ct. 30/-
9ct. 17/6
Silver 5/-

567. Solid Plain Signet. Stone or Tablet.
18ct. 32/-
15ct. 25/-
9ct. 15/6
Silver 4/6

590. Solid Plain Signet. Stone or Gold Top.
18ct. 50/-
15ct. 42/-
9ct. 23/-
Silver 5/-

Pins.

582. Horse Shoe. Pearl Set.
18ct. .. 38/-
15ct. .. 32/-
9ct. .. 19/-
Silver .. 15/-

586. Gold Cleek Pin Platinum head pearl ball. 18/6

592. Horn Pin.
18ct. .. 12/6
15ct. .. 11/-
9ct. .. 7/6
Silver .. 2/6

587. Gate Pin.
18ct. .. 12/6
15ct. .. 11/-
9ct. .. 7/6
Silver .. 2/6

Links.

620. 618.

	620.	618.
18ct.	35/-	42/-
15ct.	28/-	34/-
9ct.	15/-	18/-
Silver	4/-	5/-

570. Single Stone Diamond Claw Ring.
18ct. .. .. £5 : 0 : 0
Larger Diamond 8 : 10 : 0

Studs.

606.
18ct .. 18/-
15ct. .. 15/-

609.
9ct. .. 8/-
Silver .. 2/6

612. 613. Studs with Bead and Half-bead Tops.
612 / 613 { 18ct. 20/-
15ct. 17/-
9ct. 9/-

Ladies' Rings.

643. 18ct. five stone, half hoop.
All Diamonds 250/-
Three Diamonds and two Sapphires or Pearls 175/-
Three Diamonds and two Rubies 200/-

644. 18ct. five stone, half hoop.
All Diamonds 190/-
Three Sapphires and two Diamonds 126/-
Three Diamonds and two Pearls 150/-
Three Diamonds and two Rubies 165/-

646. 18ct. Cluster Ring.
All Diamonds 155/-
Sapphire or Pearl in centre, Diamonds round .. 110/-
Ruby centre 135/-

647. 18ct. Marquise Cluster.
All Diamonds 175/-
Diamonds and Pearl or Sapphires.. .. 130/-

648. 18ct. five stone Gipsy.
All Pearls.. .. 38/-
Diamonds & Pearls 78/-
Coral 30/-

649. 18ct. three stone, Gipsy.
Three Diamonds 105/-
One Diamond & two Rubies 75/-
One Diamond and two Pearls or Sapphires .. 58/6

653. Buckle.
18ct. 26/-
15ct. 22/-
9ct. 13/-
Silver 1/9

658. Mizpah Ring.
18ct. 27/-
15ct. 23/-
9ct. 14/-
Silver 2/6

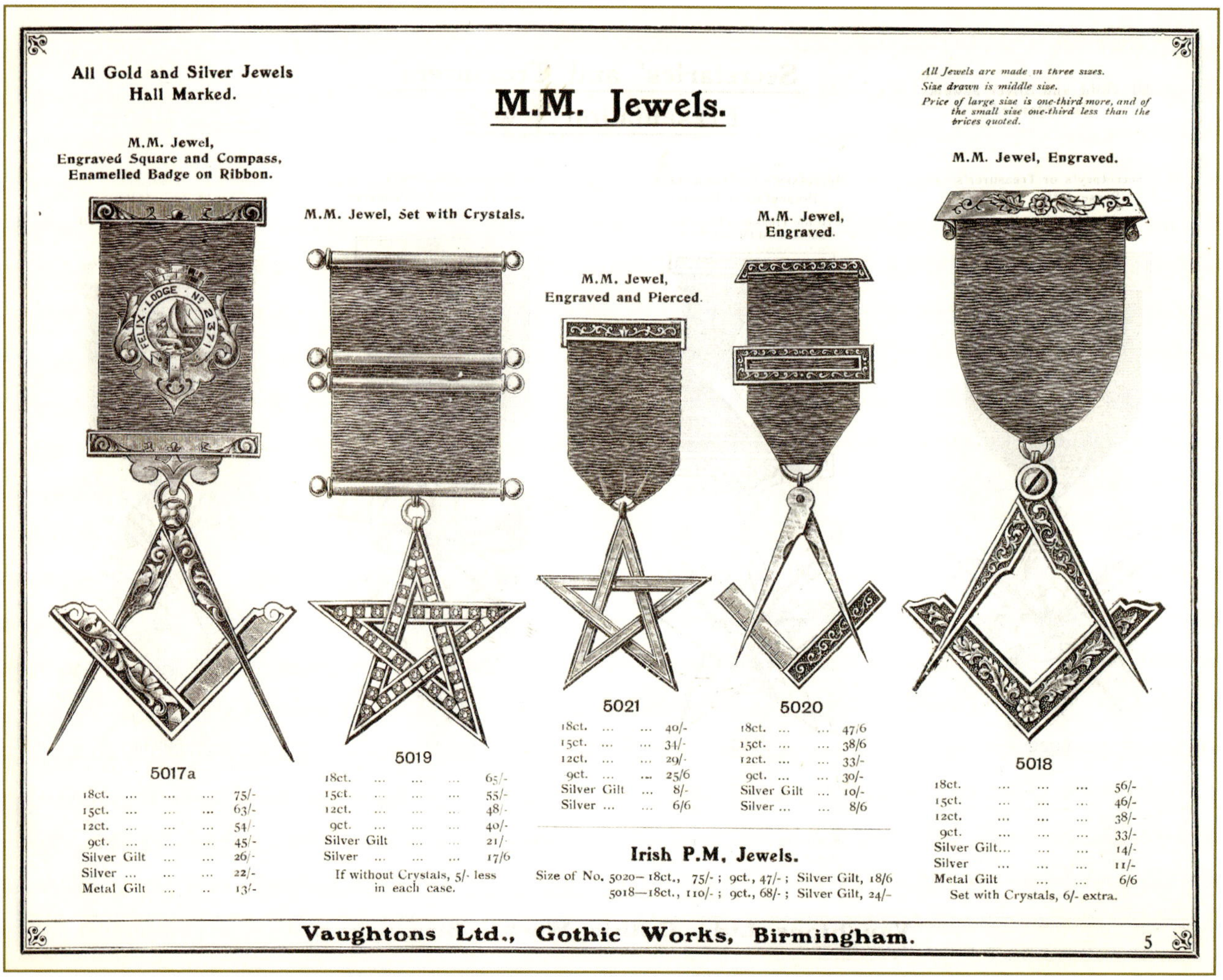

All Gold and Silver Jewels Hall Marked.

M.M. Jewels.

All Jewels are made in three sizes.
Size drawn is middle size.
Price of large size is one-third more, and of the small size one-third less than the prices quoted.

M.M. Jewel, Engraved Square and Compass, Enamelled Badge on Ribbon.

5017a

18ct.	75/-
15ct.	63/-
12ct.	54/-
9ct.	45/-
Silver Gilt	26/-
Silver	22/-
Metal Gilt	13/-

M.M. Jewel, Set with Crystals.

5019

18ct.	65/-
15ct.	55/-
12ct.	48/-
9ct.	40/-
Silver Gilt	21/-
Silver	17/6

If without Crystals, 5/- less in each case.

M.M. Jewel, Engraved and Pierced.

5021

18ct.	40/-
15ct.	34/-
12ct.	29/-
9ct.	25/6
Silver Gilt	8/-
Silver	6/6

M.M. Jewel, Engraved.

5020

18ct.	47/6
15ct.	38/6
12ct.	33/-
9ct.	30/-
Silver Gilt	10/-
Silver	8/6

M.M. Jewel, Engraved.

5018

18ct.	56/-
15ct.	46/-
12ct.	38/-
9ct.	33/-
Silver Gilt	14/-
Silver	11/-
Metal Gilt	6/6

Set with Crystals, 6/- extra.

Irish P.M. Jewels.

Size of No. 5020—18ct., 75/- ; 9ct., 47/- ; Silver Gilt, 18/6
5018—18ct., 110/- ; 9ct., 68/- ; Silver Gilt, 24/-

Vaughtons Ltd., Gothic Works, Birmingham. 5

This is by no means an exhaustive list and the more information is sought it just continues to expand the boundaries of production. Vaughtons success was very much their ongoing adoption of the latest "technologies", innovative designs and their willingness to undertake unusual work pieces. This strategy stood the company in excellent stead whilst many Birmingham and London based manufacturers of badges or those having only a limited or small product range progressively failed to survive. Many cities and regional towns had large department stores where customers would go along to order whatever was required. Vaughtons were particularly successful in getting these retailers to act as "agents" and recommend Vaughtons goods and services. Often the larger stores would have their own name stamped on the supplied goods such was their "clout".

Whilst Vaughtons did not hold the Royal Warrant, they supplied suppliers and jewellers, such as Garrards, who were such holders. There are numerous and worldwide, outstanding references to persons supplied including all of the English monarchs from Queen Victoria onwards, and overseas clients such as the Shah of Iran, many Commonwealth and Colonial dignitaries and Civic dignitaries.

The early Vaughton catalogues were simply a white frontsheet with a red logo with striking red tick followed by a simple interior design. Examples of goods were simply page laid with title and costs per piece per substrate. For handouts and fliers examples exist of royal blue printed documents of equally simple design. These were superseded circa 1902 by glossy, high quality art works with the now familiar logo, scroll decoration work, Vaughton mark and the company's latest telephone number, this established the opening of the newly constructed Gothic Works at Livery Street. An engraving of the building was incorporated into the fly piece of these later documents.

Typically when issued, three catalogues were produced; one military driven specifying the supply of goods to the military services, a Masonic catalogue and a third Specialities and Localosities catalogue.

Typically these contained 30–40 pages each side crammed with highly detailed photographs but also emphasizing that each could be hand crafted to specific customer requirements if necessary.

Medal making

The larger scale development of Vaughton medal-making began in earnest following the move to Gothic Works, since in 1909 the new company is quoted as including 'the business of Diesinkers and Stampers'. Both of these activities are essential for the production of medals and badges.

A die starts its life as a plain cylindrical, soft-steel block that, under the skilled work of a die-sinker, will eventually become the source to enable the production of medals or badges. The designs of many medals were and still are often in high relief. Work on an intricate medal can often take weeks to complete, this is also true of today's workmanship. It is implicit that to achieve such definitive relief the die-sinker has to work accurately but also "in reverse"; the deeper he goes with his engraving tools into the die body, the greater the eventual relief, and the three dimensionality and detail of the design.

At regular intervals the craftsman would press a blob of plasticine into the die to inspect his progress; removal of the blob showed the achieved finish but "looking at his work the correct way round". The craftsman repeats this process until the die was fully finished.

When finished the soft steel die was heated up in a dedicated gas fired furnace and 'hardened', so as to be able to withstand the physical pressure of the stamping process. In the case of 'badges' the die-sinking was, of course, simpler in nature, normally being uniformly shallow in depth, since the vast majority of badges would end up by being enamelled.

An operator using a 'drop stamp', perhaps in a battery of one, two or four would undertake the stamping of badges. Each drop stamp had a heavy metal piece on the end of a rope, which was manually hauled up by the operator and then allowed to drop down from a height onto a base metal blank, which had been placed on top of the die. To ease the manual effort of pulling on the rope, with hand and foot, it was made to pass over a continuously rotating overhead pulley on a spindle, which ran down the full length of the press shop. The whole system was driven by

a large electric motor. Thus all the various types of press were powered from this central source; apart from those that had their own electric motor incorporated into the design.

Simple metal pressings were produced by girls' operating hand presses and the secret for them was to remember to withdraw your hand before pulling on the metal arm of the press. Unfortunately, accidents did happen, and fingers were cut off as a result, one of the hazards of the trade. Indeed, on occasions, such as the start to Christmas or Bank Holidays, the days' work would cease at midday.

Management certainly did not want press operators to return to work in the afternoon after enjoying a convivial hour in the nearby pub!

Medal production, as distinct to simple metal lapel badges, would be a choice of using either base metal, silver, or gold blanks and this higher class of work was carried out on friction screw presses. These comprised of two vertical rotating friction discs sited on the upper part of the press, either side of a horizontal flywheel. When the revolving discs made contact with the flywheel

it caused it to revolve and screw downwards to complete the pressing process. The obverse and reverse medal dies would have a metal, silver or gold blank placed between them, with a metal collar to hold everything in place, and to enable the finished medal to have a raised rim surround. Often the rim would be serrated at a later date.

The press operator was a skilled craftsman since a delicate touch was required in setting-up the operation, controlling the up and downward slide movement, and deciding the actual stamping power and depth required from the press. This was a critical judgement, get it wrong and the valuable handmade steel dies could be split asunder. But if all went well the eventual medal recipients would possess what has been termed as, 'a piece of hand held sculpture'.

The original design for such as Coronation medals was often sculpted by well-known artists. Designers such as Bertram Mac Kennel and Alfred Toft, extremely well established in their age and both responsible for sculptures still highly regarded in Birmingham were two such individuals known to design medals (and coins).

To obtain the various diameters of medals necessitates that the original large bronze model was placed on a reducing pantograph. This is an instrument with jointed rods often used for copying drawings, but to a different scale. By adjusting the rods the scale of the image produced can be changed. The medallist can use the same principle of the reducing pantograph for engraving a steel die, with a cutter revolving at high speed replacing a drawing implement. The tracing pointer on the pantograph slowly moves in ever-decreasing circles over the artist's mould. Initially the pointer used would have a large head, so that the mere outline of the design can be cut. Gradually, with each succeeding cut, the pointer used will become more 'pointed'; so that by the final cut every fine detail of the original sculpture is faithfully reproduced. It is a lengthy process, taking perhaps one or two weeks of constant cutting. And as the final cuts approach it is absolutely vital that the pantograph machine does not suffer from any shakes or jolts, or a blemish would appear on the steel die.

The original Livery Street Gothic Works pantograph machine was situated near to the Press Shop; these final cuts were often undertaken overnight, when all other machinery nearby had been shut down.

1908 Olympics

The 1908 Olympics were held in London and Vaughtons were commissioned to undertake the medals, badges and associated ephemera. For such a prestigious event the designs were formally completed by "Bertram" MacKennal. Sir Edgar George MacKennal KCVO was a designer and sculptor of international renown. He most famously designed coinage bearing the head of King George V.

Below is a Judges Badge, again stuck by Vaughtons. The badge was produced in pressed silvered metal and enamel and shows the head of Athena surrounded by "Olympic Games, London, 1908, Judge", again designed by MacKennal, the reverse show the quadriga winning a chariot race.

The medal below is a Participation Medal, it shows a winged figure of Victory, the reverse shows a Quadriga winning a chariot race. A quadriga is a team of four horses abreast drawing a chariot.

The medal below is a gold prize winner's medal awarded to an unknown Australian rugby player. It was produced in 15 carat gold. The obverse side shows two maidens crowning a victorious athlete. The reverse side shows St George slaying a dragon. The Australian team won the final 32–3 beating the Great Britain team; essentially on this occasion this was the Cornish Rugby side.

Below is a photograph of the complete set of medals along with their presentation boxes. The medals are inscribed as follows; -

Winner, Water Polo.

Charles Sidney Smith, Olympic Games, Winner, Water Polo, 1908. This was presented to Smith who went on to win back to back medals in the following 1912 Olympics. He returned to the sport aged 41 to win a third gold in the 1920 Olympics held in Antwerp. In 1912 he became the first invited athlete to carry team flag at the Opening Ceremony.

Second Prize Running Dear Teams.

Dear Running was one of 15 events in the shooting program. The Great Britain Team consisted of four marksmen, Charles Nix, William Russell Layne –Joynt, Walter Ellicot and Ted Ranken. A deer shaped target made 10 runs of 75 feet, each run lasting around 4 seconds. Each competitor was allowed 1 shot per run at a distance of 110 yards. Concentric circles were drawn on the target deer ranging from a 1 to 4 score. Great Britain narrowly missed out on the gold, accumulating 1 point less than the winning Sweden Team.

Third Prize Bantam Boxing.

The bronze was won by William "Wally" Webb of Great Britain. He was born in November 1882 and affiliated to the 17th. North Middlesex School of Arms Amateur Boxing Club.

The 3 medals sold at a Sotheby's auction in July 2012 for £17,000.

The medal on the right shows the first silver awarded for a Winter Olympics sport. It shows

again two maidens crowning a victorious winner and St George slaying a dragon. The medal is believed to be that awarded to Arthur Cummings who finished second in the Special Figure Ice Skating competition. Tragically Cummings was involved in a motorcycle accident in 1914 and died a day later of tetanus on his 25th birthday.

The photograph below shows a fine quality silver inkpot mounted with two enamelled roundels, these being coloured with artistic interpretations of the Participation Medal design. Again this was produced by Vaughtons and is of square form, engraved monograms on sides between enamel roundels, it has a hinged lid with a Tudor Rose design, blue glass liner and green baize underside, height approx. 31/2 inches.

Commemorative Spoons

Commemorative Spoons have long been a forte in Vaughton's portfolio.

Many were produced with civic and armorial designs as mementoes of visiting towns and cities, presentations to dignitaries, as celebrations of anniversaries or centenaries or presentations for services. Spoons were often produced in sets, especially so for fraternal and Masonic societies, the later having the Masonic symbol for each serving officer embossed into the spoon handle.

Spoons have been produced for numerous Royal occaisions such as weddings, jubilees, ascensions, investitures and sadly deaths.

Most recently spoons were presented to the Pope on his visit to Birmingham in 2012. As shown below sets were produced in Papal Purple and Cardinal Red. Approximately 1500 sets of spoons were produced to celebrate this event.

Vehicle Badges

Vaughtons have long had a history in the supply of badges, bracketry, fittings and fixtures and associated automotive components, the latter mainly in pressed steel. An extensive range of automotive sectors were supplied including car, bicycle and motorcycle, heavy vehicle and bus badges. The following poster shows a typical variety of badges supplied to the trade.

In time these were supplemented by society badges and ephemera including cuff links and tie bars, all showing the badges of the originator.

Triumph Medal; The medal below shows an example of the ongoing association with the automotive sector; it is

Illustrations of a few Radiator, Dashboard and Direction Plates. High-class Vitreous Enamelled Radiator Plates a Specialty. Free Quotations for all kinds of Stamped and Press Work, Toolmaking, etc.

date 1919 and was presented apparently as an "apprentice award"

The following plates show illustrations from catalogues showing the various simple and complex pressings and assemblies; the first showing so called "raised articles" the latter round washes in many of their forms.

The following sheets are taken from the 1905 catalogue and show the diversity of pressed metal ware produced at the time. The complex forms show the skills used at a time when presses where much simpler than today.

Vaughtons produced many forms of washers, many of which were produce from hand driven ball presses. The worker placed the metal piece into a jig which was then fixed. The press head was swung through 180 degrees, the weight of a large metal ball driving a screw thread which in turn pushed a die into the metal to cut and pierce it. The process was repeated endlessly with thousands of washers being produced daily.

Many workers developed a "musculature" to their preferred arm, the repeated swinging of the ball weighted head giving them great strength in that arm. Some of the heavier balls weighted around 15 kilograms, imaging doing that 50 times a minute over an eight hour working day.

Vaughtons local involvements were recorded especially so in the bicycle and tricycle industrial sectors with specific presence at large exhibitions. Speedwell Bicycle Club was probably the earliest and certainly the most prestigious of such clubs in Birmingham. It was founded in 1876 its headquarters were in Edgbaston's Speedwell Road. Five annual exhibitions devoted primarily to cycles were organised by the Speedwell Club during the 1880s, the first one in March 1882.

Vaughtons were present at the Speedwell Club Bicycle Exhibition, held at Bingley hall Birmingham in March 1882 along with *"60 exhibitors. In addition there were long and important arrays of ordinary horse drawn carriages of various kinds shown by Messrs Startin and Sons and well known other coachbuilders"*…. at the time providing Cycle Club badges and other items. Other exhibitors at that venue includes Singer & Co., the Caroche Tricycle Co., the Manchester Tricycle Co., the Swallow Bicycle and Tricycle Co., the Centaur Cycle Co and a local manufacture of some later note, BSA. A 1909 advertisement actually includes Cycle Name Plates as one of the Gothic Works major product lines, the badge accompanying the advert shows the badge of the "Wolverhampton Automobile Club".

This automotive link has recently been exemplified in the latest range of badges supplied to Aston Martin and their recent catalogues.

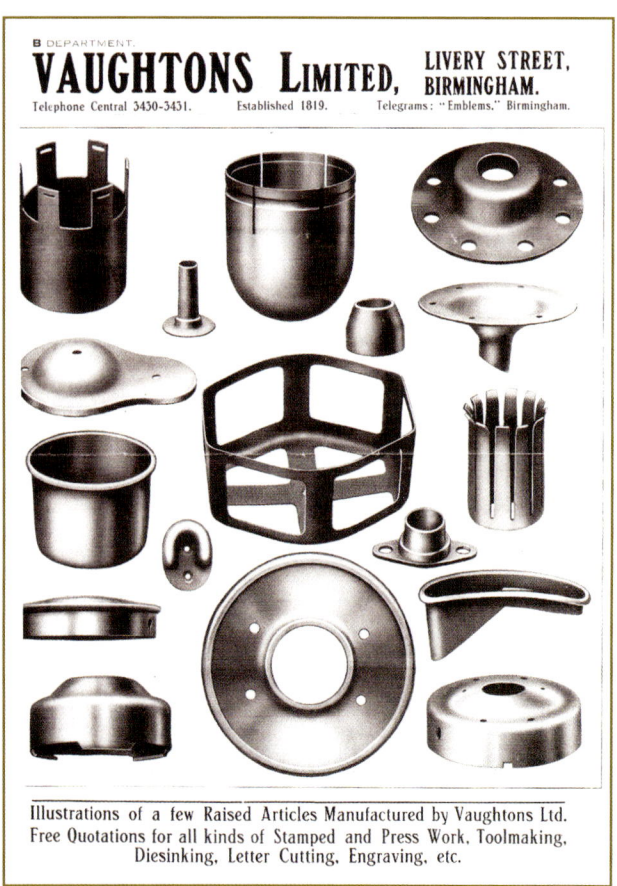

Illustrations of a few Raised Articles Manufactured by Vaughtons Ltd.
Free Quotations for all kinds of Stamped and Press Work, Toolmaking, Diesinking, Letter Cutting, Engraving, etc.

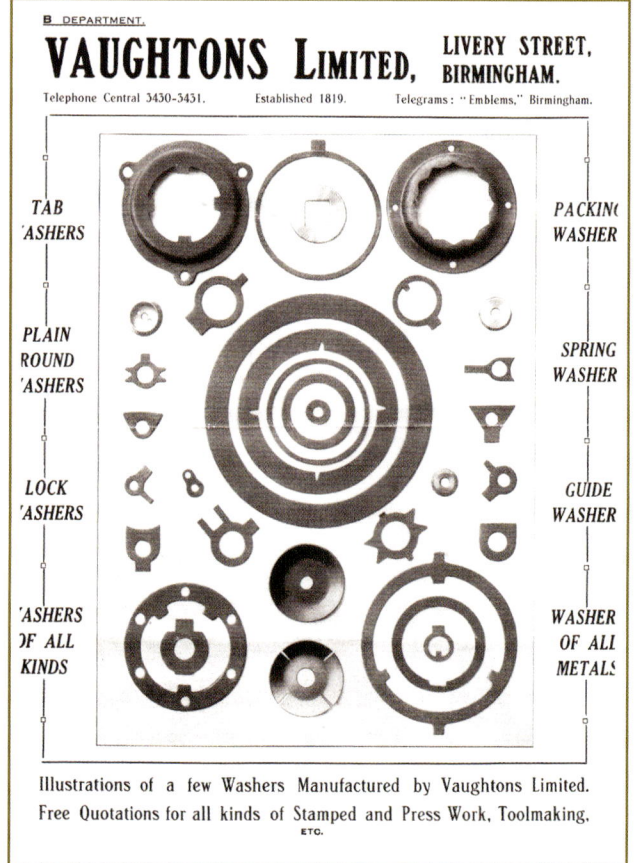

Illustrations of a few Washers Manufactured by Vaughtons Limited.
Free Quotations for all kinds of Stamped and Press Work, Toolmaking, ETC.

In addition, medals were struck in 2012 for the Jenson Motors Anniversary and E–Type Jaguar Anniversary.

Aston Martin was founded in 1913 by Lionel Martin and Robert Bamford. The two had joined forces as Bamford & Martin the previous year to sell cars made by Singer from premises in Callow Street, London where they also serviced GWK and Calthorpe vehicles to support their future plans . Martin raced specials at Aston Hill near Aston Clinton, and the pair eventually decided to make their own vehicles. The first car to bear the full name Aston Martin was created by Martin by fitting a four-cylinder Coventry-Simplex engine to the chassis of a 1908 Isotta-Fraschini.

Jensen Motors Ltd was a British manufacturer of sports cars and commercial vehicles, based in West Bromwich, west of Birmingham. The company was established in 1934 and ceased trading in 1976. The medal struck marked the company's 75th. Anniversary. In 1934 they were commissioned by American film actor Clark Gable to design and build a car for him based on a Ford chassis.

The Jaguar E-Type was a British sports car, manufactured by Jaguar Cars Ltd between 1961 and 1974. Its combination of iconic styling and good looks, high performance and competitive pricing established the marque as the dream car of 1960s motoring. More than 70,000 E-Types were sold. The 40th. Anniversary medal was struck as a commemorative item.

The photograph bellows the exceptional workmanship of Vaughton's craftsmen. It is the medal awarded at the Franco–British Exhibition of 1908. It was designed by F Bowcher, another of Vaughton's associations, and shows Britannia and another symbolic figure conversing, overlooked by a winged figure. The inscription; London MDCCCVIII is shown around the top edge. The medal was awarded for "Violin and case". The medal was produced in silver and has a 52 mm diameter

The plate below and on page 32 show the outstanding silverware being produced by the company; they show a 1929 speedboat and its driver mounted on a "seascape" base.

The plates below show the outstanding medals also being produced.

The plate atop the page shows a medal produced for the Worshipful Company of Scriveners; this is an outstanding example of a multi part/multi die jewel that was cut to shape and featuring vitreous enamels and hand painted detail. The medal is Stone Set.

The medal on the lower left shows a President's Medal from the Stonehaven Burns Club; it is hand painted and hangs from a double mitred ribbon.

The lower right plate shows a medal presented to the Chartered Institute of Highways and Transportation and is a fine example of a saw pierced and hand painted jewel.

The plate opposite show that all activities were catered for. Hand-bell tune ringing in any town is very ancient, probably going back at least to the 1700s and earlier, along with many other towns and villages especially so amongst the Pennines.

The following photograph shows Huddersfield Band, winners of the 1904 British Open which was the Golden Jubilee of the hand-bell competitions held at Belle Vue. A special Medal was produced by Vaughtons to commemorate this.

The Jubilee competition had 16 bands in the line-up. The band brought in a paid conductor J. B "Wick" Lodge, whose ability to conduct hand-bells was renowned. He was also a tower bell ringer at Huddersfield Parish Church, and lived at 3 Commercial Place, (next to the canal) Commercial Street, which runs from the University to Firth Street.

The test piece was Verdi's "Rigoletto". The band returned to Huddersfield and marched from the railway station to their headquarters in Battye's Yard off the Market Place in triumph. That year they had won the double–The Yorkshire Championship and the British Open.

There were twelve members in the band. In honour of the Jubilee, it is thought that every member of the band received one of the special medals, as an identical one was featured in the Examiner in the 1980s from the family of J. B Lodge.

The following two photographs show original workbooks retrieved from storage at the Well Street premises; these show the original drawings, diagrams, all pasted into everyday working formats. This is where the craftsman transferred the "fag packet" ideas to formalised working job sheets. Many pieces are just loose leaf, postcards, scraps of paper; all were added into these books to be become a drawing from which the concept was converted to metal.

The workbooks date back to 1895. The masonic drawings shown in two of the books were sent to Grand Lodge as reference works and formed part of the recent "Manufacturing and Masonry Exhibition" held at Grand Lodge, London. The books are "worthless", in that they were no more than old notes, but also "priceless" in that they show how original designs were put together; in effect around 120 years of medal design were still available for study.

Within the workbooks are contained highly detailed drawings and traceries of specific elements of the design.

The following photographs show pencil and pen traceries of specific elements of the designs manufactured.

All of the annotations were hand inscribed and corrected, the original Vaughton drawings were also copied by other companies in this case T J Shelton.

On page 36 is a typical hand annotated job card with instructions for alterations to the design produced to date.

The 3 items on page 36 are chroma, water washed hand paintings on cardboard bases. The first showing Wiltshire Football Association Chairman's medal, the second showing a Rotary International Honorary Treasure design; both are the final design approval sheets. The Institution of Gas Engineers design has some hand annotations on the reverse. These to be completed as instructed.

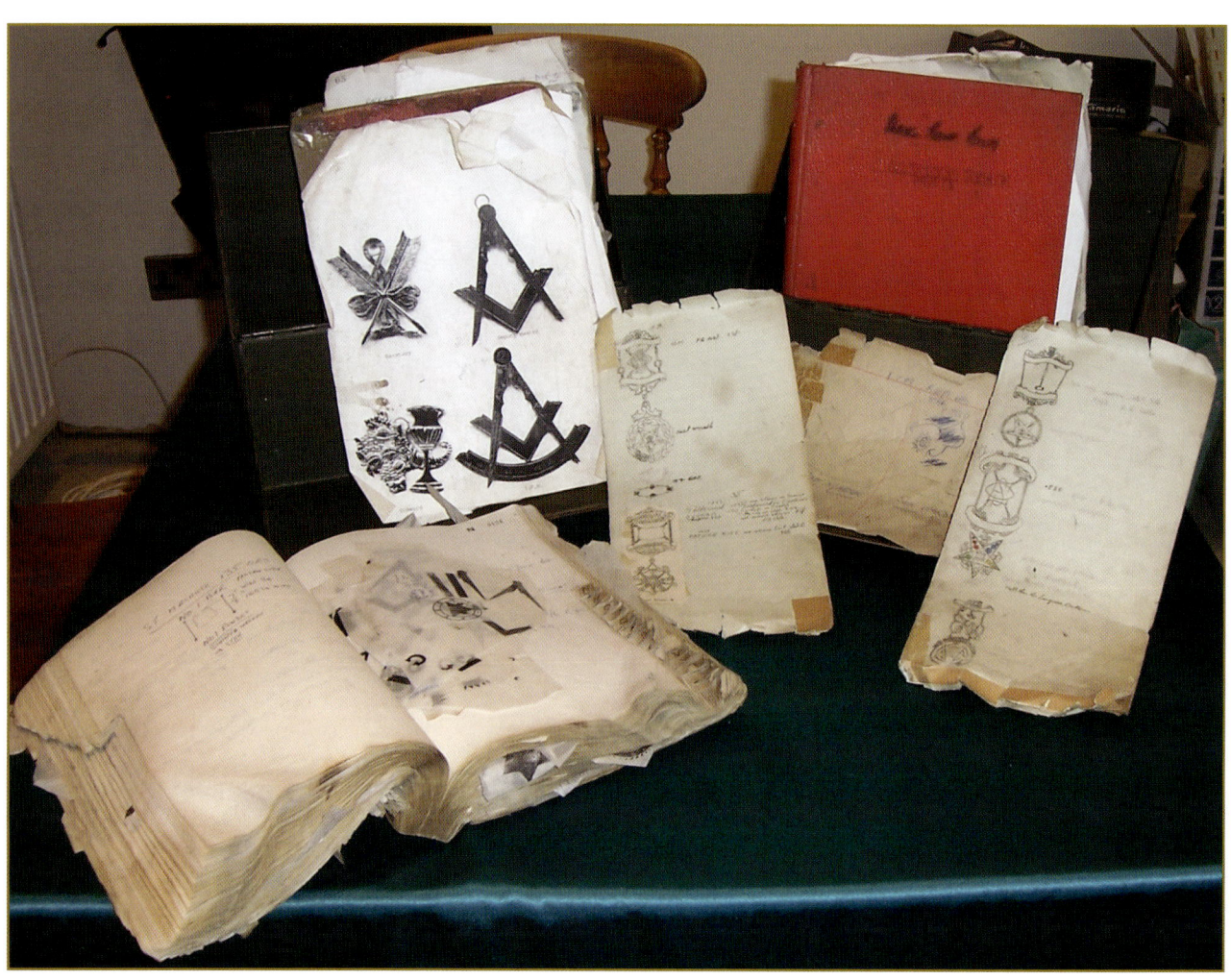

THE BOOK OF
PUBLIC ARMS
D 1950
1951

D59
D58
D57
D56
T. J. SKELTON

D51
D52
D53
D54
D55
T.J. SKELTON.

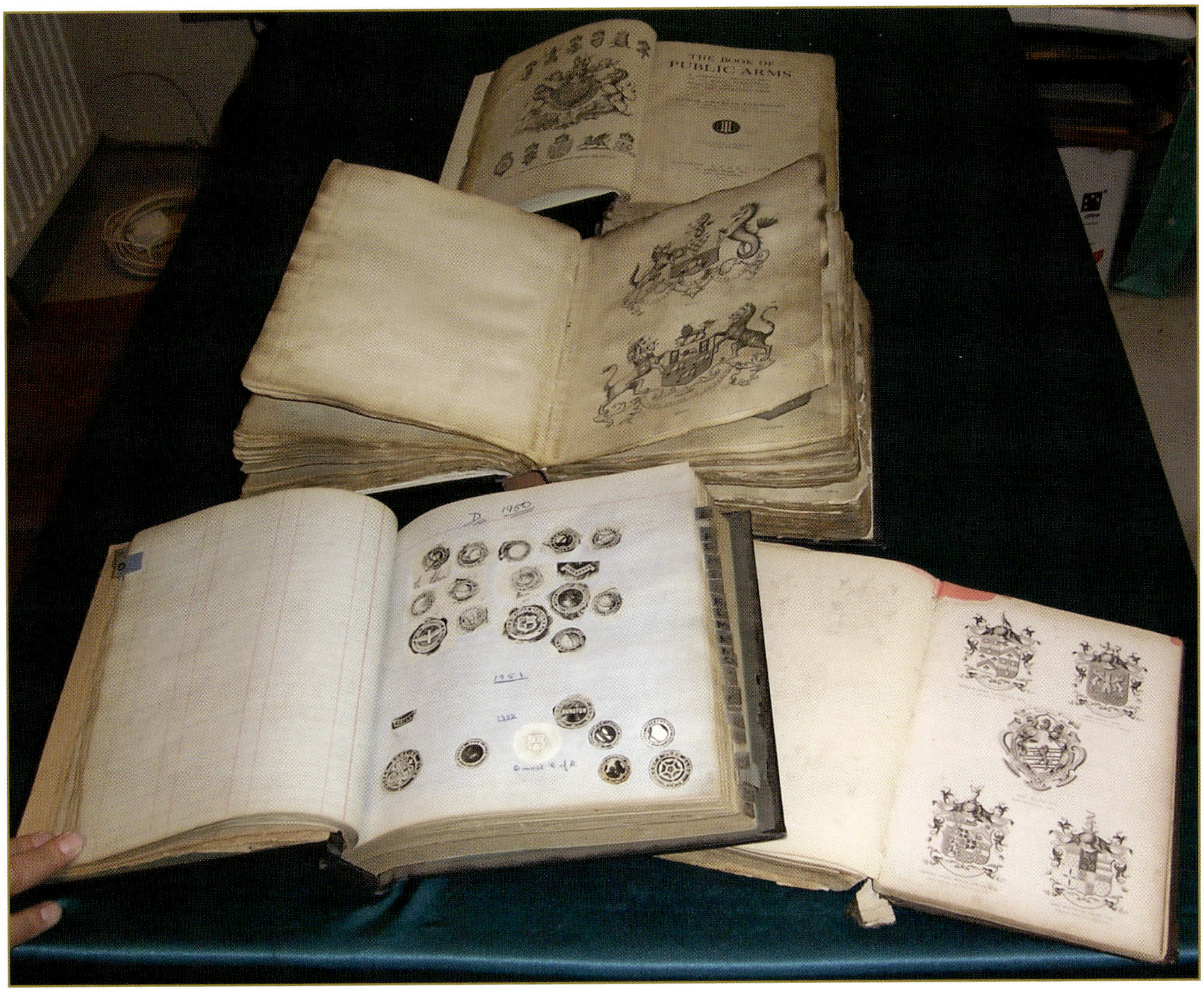

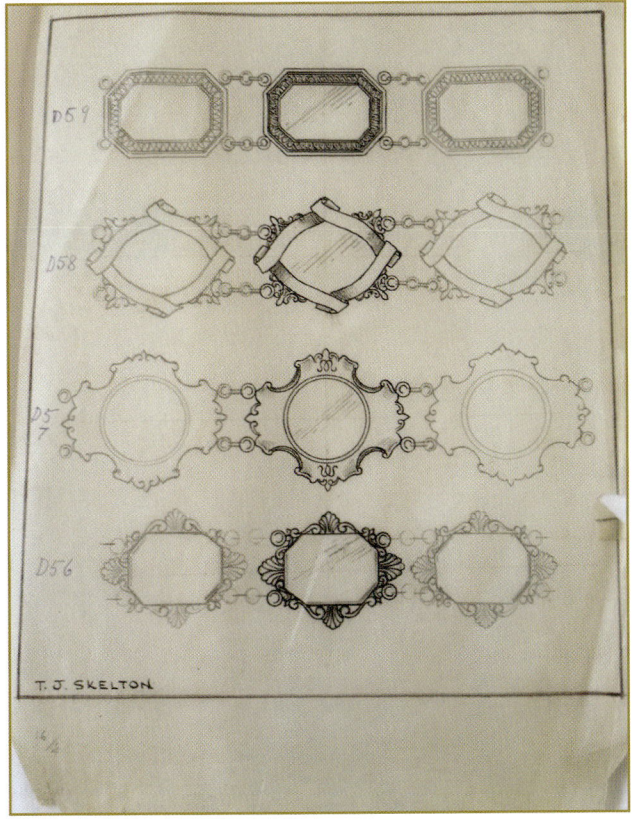

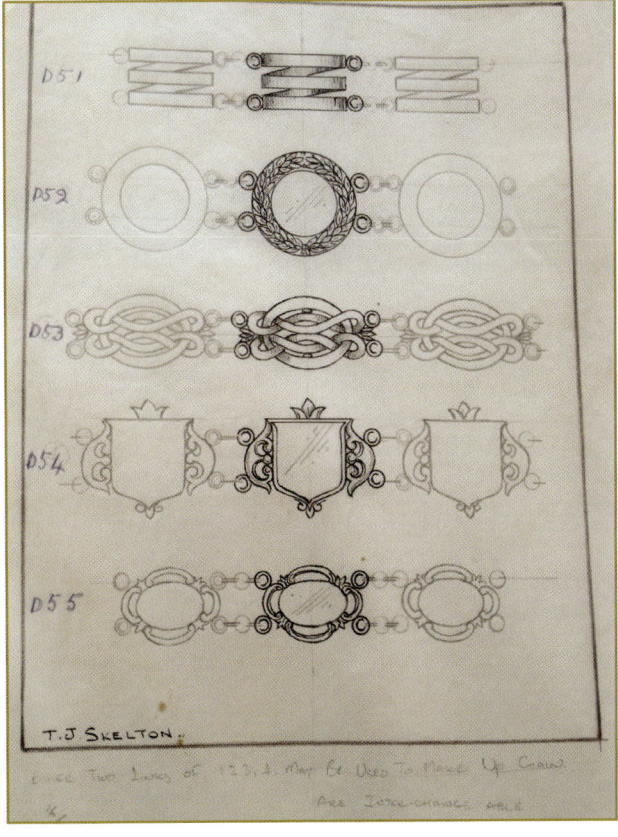

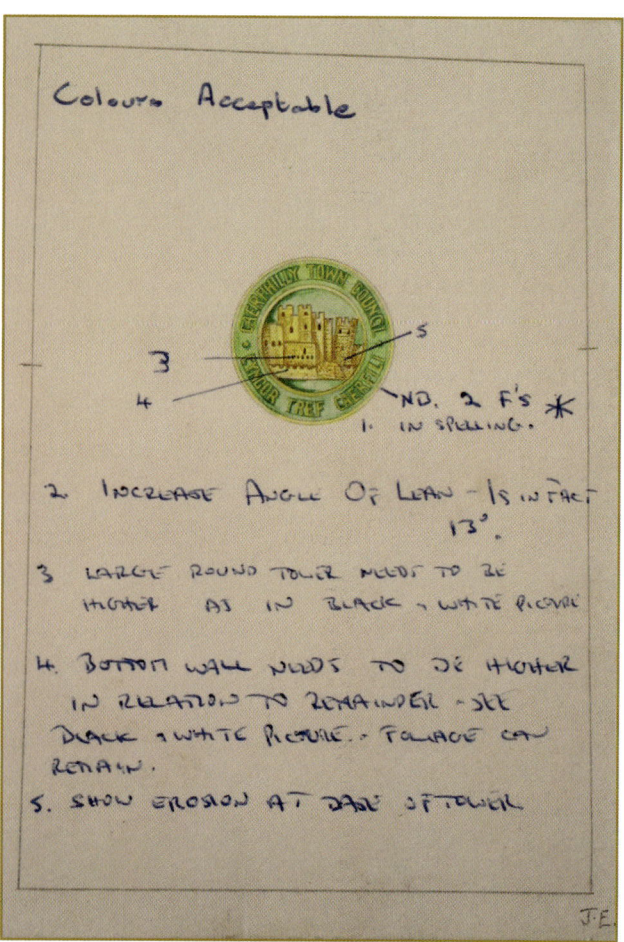

Colours Acceptable

3

4

ND. 2 F's ✱
1. IN SPELLING.

2 INCREASE ANGLE OF LEAN - IS IN FACT 13°.

3 LARGE ROUND TOWER NEEDS TO BE HIGHER AS IN BLACK & WHITE PICTURE

4. BOTTOM WALL NEEDS TO BE HIGHER IN RELATION TO REMAINDER - SEE BLACK & WHITE PICTURE - FOLIAGE CAN REMAIN.

5. SHOW EROSION AT BASE OF TOWER

J.E.

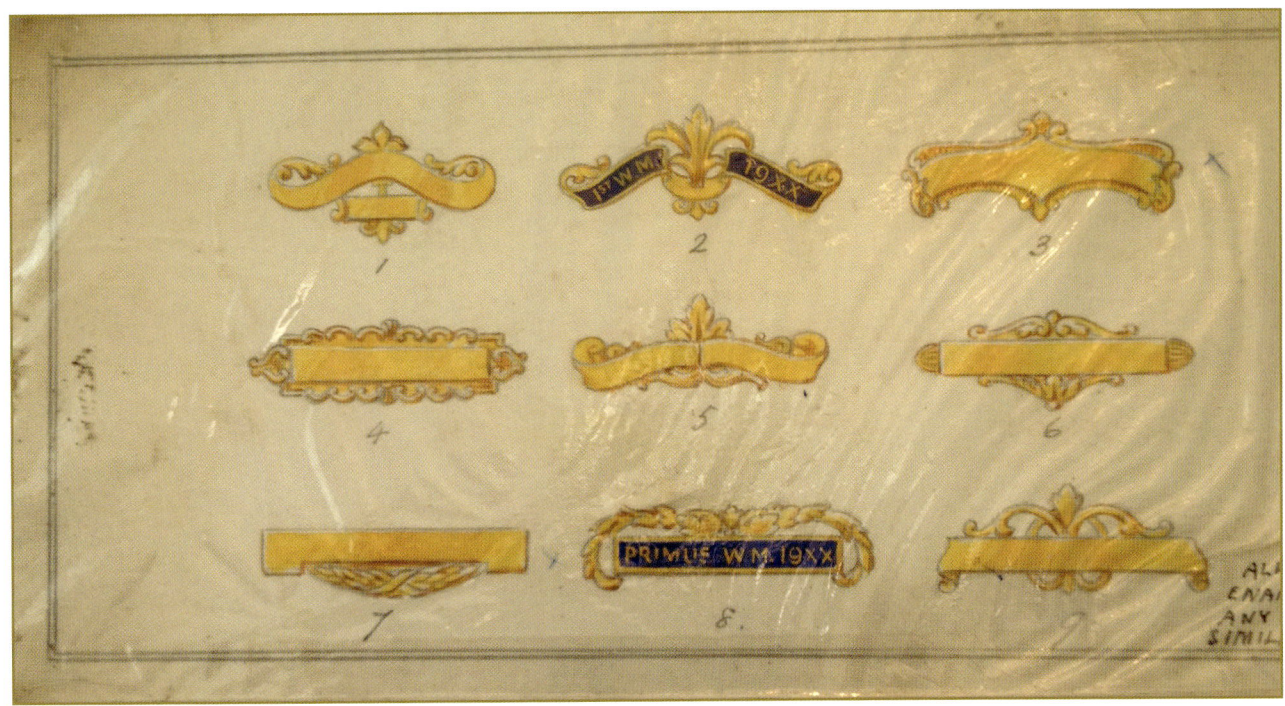

The card above shows a hand drawn salesman's card for him or her to illustrate the bars, used to adorn medals and jewels, which the client could adopt or use for the basis of his custom design.

The small hand painted card below shows a design presented to Galashiels, along with the annotations for final completion.

The card below show a litho printed design again with the recipients comments for completion

On page 38, this "dog eared" fragment was cut and pasted from book of heraldic designs and passed to the designer on which to base his piece. Hundreds of these fragments exist although to which jewel or medal they inspired is not always

VIVIT · POST · FUNERA · VIRTUS

recorded. The Vaughton Archive contains at two complete volumes of heraldic designs, one for every city and major town in the United Kingdom. Almost every page has holes were the workman cut and then pasted the design onto a job card from which a medal or piece was then produced.

Top left of page 39 is an Institute of Bankers design with ringed centre where the heraldic crest was incorrect and had to be replaced, note the simplicity of the design, this would have been probably a "first" draft (paper then stuck onto a cardboard base. Top right of page 39 is one of 3 designs submitted as possible medals for the Past Sherriff of Chester, again the simplicity of the design suggests a "first" draft.

The bottom left picture on page 39 is a Showmans Guild–Yorkshire Section Chairman's Medal. The design within the centre was obtained from a photograph obtained at the time from a local paper hence the detail of the "helter skelter". The White Rose is of course the County Flower.

The bottom right picture on page 39 shows how complex some of Vaughtons work could be.

Inst of Bankers

3.

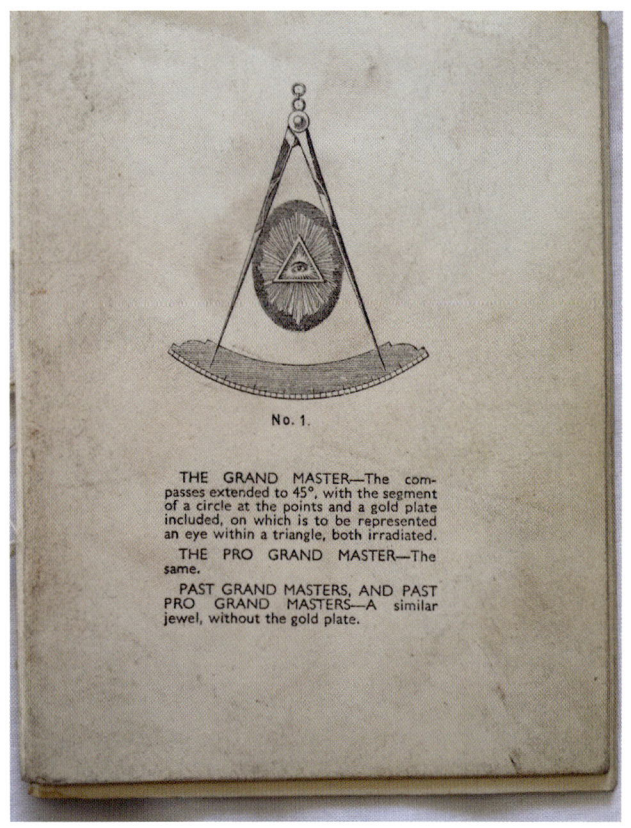

No. 1.

THE GRAND MASTER—The compasses extended to 45°, with the segment of a circle at the points and a gold plate included, on which is to be represented an eye within a triangle, both irradiated.
THE PRO GRAND MASTER—The same.
PAST GRAND MASTERS, AND PAST PRO GRAND MASTERS—A similar jewel, without the gold plate.

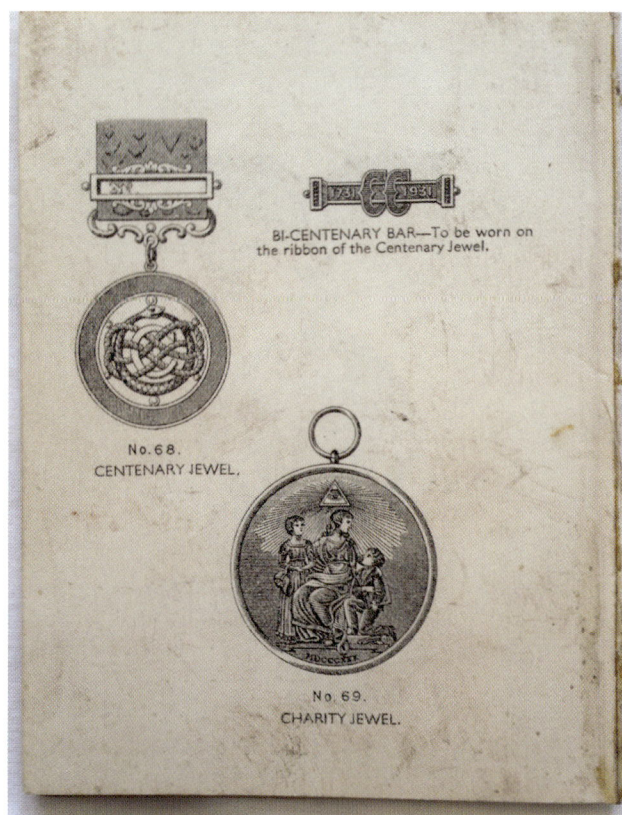

BI-CENTENARY BAR—To be worn on the ribbon of the Centenary Jewel.

No. 68.
CENTENARY JEWEL.

No. 69.
CHARITY JEWEL.

These two small books above were found in a workman's draw. They are examples of what could be handed to potential clients, in this case Freemasons. The designs are complex and the radiant eye in design No. 1 reflects a highly indented design.

In a lesser vein, the British Isles Indoor Bowel Council design (paper on cardboard base) shows how a simple design could be equally effective, even if the designer got the colour of the thistle flower wrong.

BRITISH ISLES INDOOR BOWLS COUNCIL

N/B Rose Should be yellow

Purple

The photographs opposite show:

1 This sheet of tracery over cardboard shows the Eastleigh Amateur Swimming Association Past president medal; hand painted colour wash over pencil and pen layout with pencil drawn annotations.

2 Almost complete; a fully finished jewel still attached to its job card.

3 Fully complete; a fully finished jewel still attached to its job card. This is a jewel for the Knight of Red Cross Constantine, die reference 06638, produced in 1956; note the pen written annotations.

4 Fully complete; a fully finished jewel still attached to its job card. This is a jewel for the London Albert Edward Lodge No. 592; note the pen written annotations. Note the use or recycled job cards. The left hand shows "composites" cut and pasted from a previous job with upper and lower bars and the square and compass. The blank between the two bars was pasted in "for sizing".

1

2

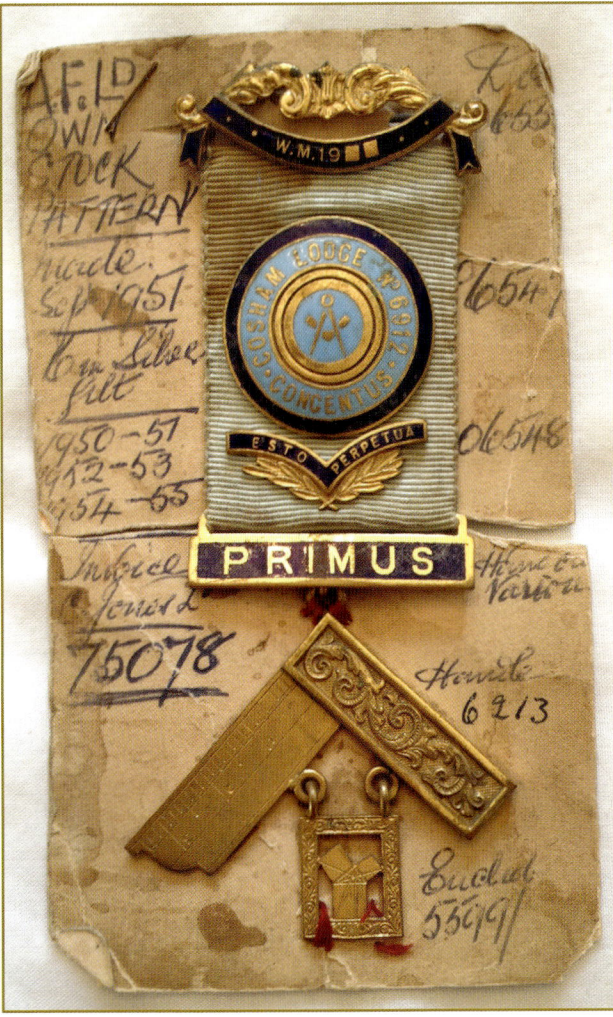

3

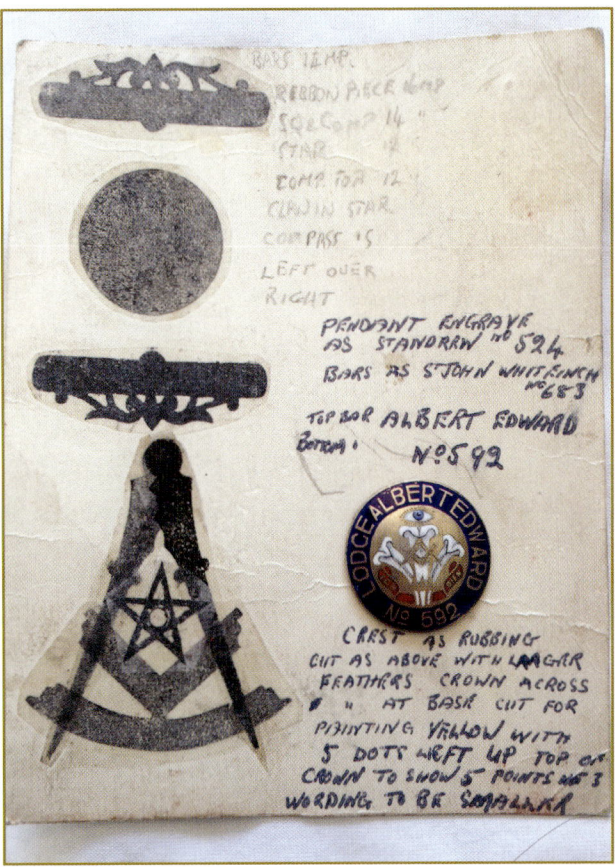

4

The final product and an example of a packaging box. The two items are not connected but were found together.

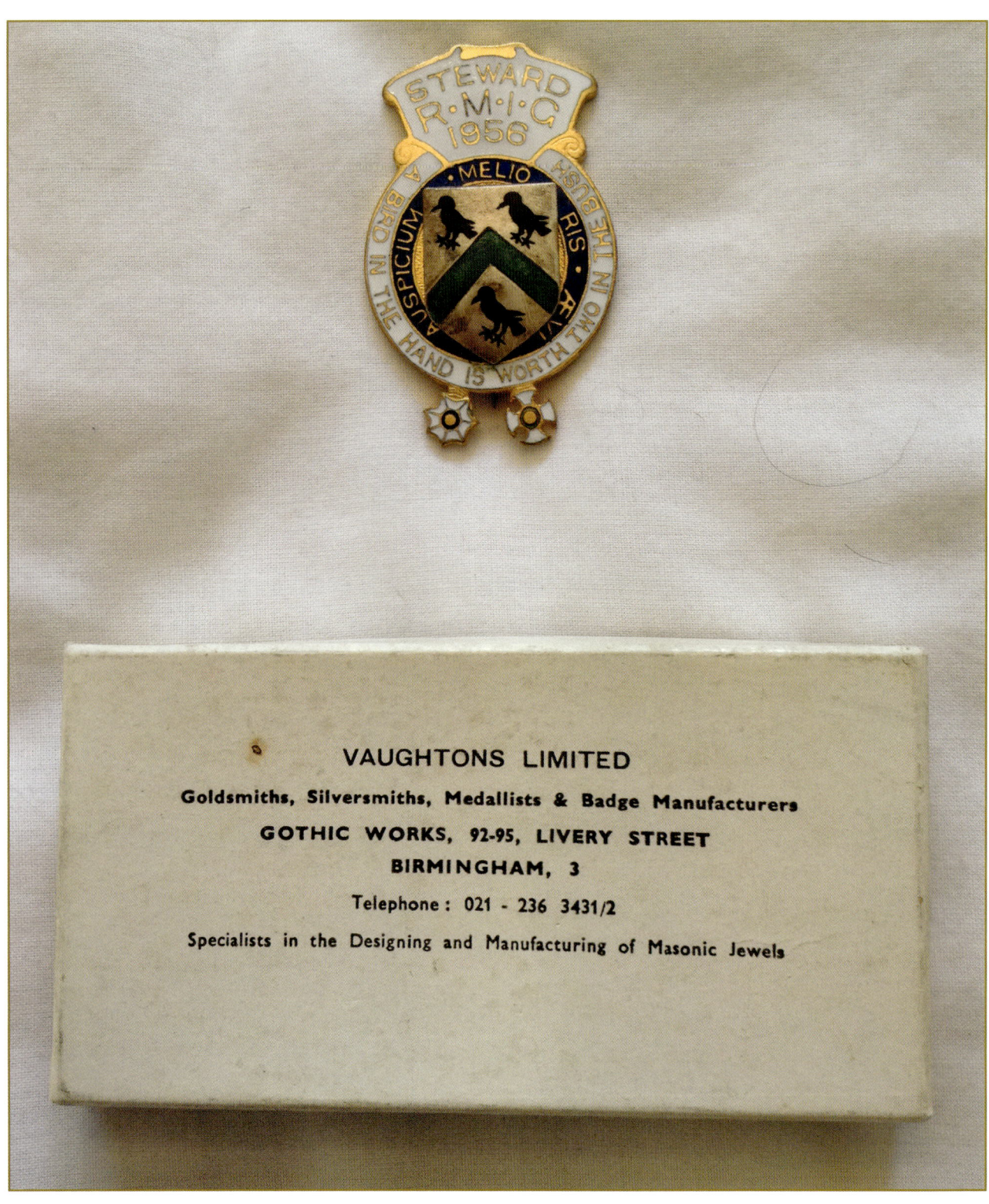

CHAPTER FIVE – WORKING AT VAUGHTONS

Under the heading 'Vaughton Gothic Works' there is mention of the new building in a Birmingham Civic Society newsletter. To this day it is an impressive building, and noted in particular were 'its excellent terracotta details, especially the lettering'. The architect in 1902 was Sidney Herbert Vaughton (born 1869); obviously keeping the work in the family!

Brian Vaughton recalls working at the company, 1949-1967, *"there were two separate departments, A & B. 'A' department, which I was mainly concerned with, was involved with a wide range of medal & badge making, mayoral chains, trophy cups and tankards, challenge shields and plaques, Masonic jewellery and presentation keys etc., a whole range of metal, silver or gold ware. 'B' department was mainly concerned with metal pressings of every description, ranging from aero-engine parts to bits and pieces for coal-mining machinery."*

"Apart from such pressings, 'B' department also produced the medal and badge pressings, which were then passed to 'A' department for enamelling, engraving, silver or gold plating, and final polishing. For instance, we made gold medals for the Football League winners and also presentation medals for a vast number of amateur sporting clubs such as the large Derbyshire Amateur Football League down to the Cradley Heath Football League, in the depths of the Black Country. However, in both cases, the presentation of the awards were a high point in their respective seasons".

"Whilst Gothic Works was operational it housed the management offices at the front of the building, plus an extensive showroom. Outside his room, with its steel security gate, there was a large oval display unit housing an impressive selection of some of the medals and badges produced by the firm. I believe that this display may now be in the hands of the Birmingham City Museum."

"With regard to how the management structure changed through the family, and then to a limited company; until being sold off I recall the following."

"After Oliver Howard Vaughton (my grandfather), Philip Vaughton, and Frederick Vaughton had retired, my father Howard George Vaughton took over the helm. His sisters, Annie, May, Aileen, Doris and Grace were directors, and I joined them on the Board after a few years. My brother John came into the firm for a few years, working in 'B' Dept. before moving on to become an apprentice at BSA, and then subsequently moved on to other positions in industry."

"Although I spent 18 years with the company, leaving in 1966, I was, at heart, not a business person. Already I had begun to dabble in freelance endeavours, such as feature writing and documentary broadcasting, perhaps taking on some of the artistic genes of my grandfather on my mother's side of the family, Thomas Anderton".

"The company was sold and, according to a Birmingham Civic Society article, the firm remained at Gothic Works until 1997, when fellow trophy manufacturer W H Darby acquired the firm and transferred it to their premises at 16 Well Street in Hockley. Therefore, although 'Vaughtons' still operates today, no member of the family now owns a share in the company".

Brian and John Vaughton still maintain their records and several of the photographs and items included herein were soured from their archives.

Custom and Mal–Practice

One aspect of manufacturing articles in precious metals is the amount of dust, swarf and filings that naturally occur when a craftsman is fashioning a piece. As a consequence of this, at the end of every working day a significant amount of gold and silver scrap collects around each workbench, or falls down on to the floor beneath. Although the floors were swept on a daily basis, the residue was not merely dumped in a dustbin. In the Jewellery Quarter all leftovers are carefully collected because this dust and debris was worth money! The dust and debris could contain gold, silver, platinum, rhodium, rhenium and other precious and semi precious metals. These dusts were collected and sent back for recovery and refining for use again and there are still small refiners doing the same work today within the Jewellery Quarter. Assaying these materials used small ceramic crucibles and lead oxide as the amalgamating medium. The assay method was a standard and is still used in the London Metal Exchange processing of materials. Having worked in such an analytical house, the year's accumulated assayed scraps were collected and many a Christmas Party paid for from the hundreds of crucibles each containing a minute amount of these precious fractions.

Furthermore, at the end of each day, when the workers' washed their hands before heading for home, they may have pulled the plug up to empty their basin of water, but the liquid is directed through vats before being allowed to enter the city sewerage system. The residue settled to the bottom of the vats, and again was sent at intervals for refining so that the maximum recovery of the precious metals contained in the waste was achieved, which forms the basis for the payment to be made.

However human nature being what it is and was, sometimes less than 100% honest, there have been rare cases of jewellery craftsmen trying to take advantage of the system. For many years in the 20th century 'Brylcreem' (pronounced Brill-cream') was the well-known brand name of a men's hair grooming product. It gave the hair the then desirable shiny 'wet' look. Famous personalities such as Denis Compton, one of England's greatest batsmen, endorsed 'Brycleem'. Indeed, it made him one of the first media figures. Persons who worked at Livery Street recall a case of a male employee who applied 'Brylcreem' too but, as soon as he reached his house each evening he washed his hair. And he, too, did not allow the water to go down the drain direct. He also saved it, in order to eventually make some money out of the residue that had settled in the bottom of his basin. And this was achieved as a result of him pressing his hands into the precious metal residue on his work-bench at the end of each working day, then proceeding to run his hands through his 'Brylcreemed' hair, to which the residue stuck. Therefore, he left work each evening with, literally, a price on his head! Until, that is, the law caught up with him!

Even before Brylcreem, jewellery quarter workers were known to rub lard into their hair to achieve the same results, hence the old fashioned term 'Lardies' were referring to Birmingham workers.

The following photographs show the workspace of the current workforce, not that different from 200 years ago. It takes about 7 years to "graduate" from apprentice to craftsman and a further 7 years to end up as the principle in a workshop. 14 years to glean the skills necessary to maintain the standards required by the industry. In many cases designs are maintained wholly in the "head" of the principle, nothing is written or drafted until the initial designs have been considered…. Early workbooks from the late 1800s and 1900s show "pasted" hand drawn diagrams of what was required, literally put together on "the back of a fag packet" or on simple "postcards. From these simple designs came some of the most exquisitely complex and intricate fully finished pieces. Some still require explanation of how they were produced; not only blind soldered on one side but on two; how this is done has long remained a trade secret.

Workers took out their "space" and paid accordingly; those who did not meet the required standards of the day were literally "a waste of space" and dismissed accordingly, there replacement then taking over from where they left off… .

Good Days and then.

It was not entirely unknown for process chemicals and solutions to find their way to the drainage system, especially so when working in Livery Street in its basement. A former employee recalls, *"it was not unknown for us to drop acids down to the drain, this in itself was not rare. I can recall one day that having disposed of spent sulphuric acid that in error this was followed by a gold cyanide solution. The chemistry was instantaneous and fumes of "prussic acid" gas whisped out in profusion. There was an immediate evacuation of the entire premises. The whole building stenched of bitter almonds… ."*

"Admonishment was swiftly dealt to the unfortunate individual… but not for the pollution or health and safety issue but the fiscal loss of the gold component of the cyanide solution, around £80s" he recalls.

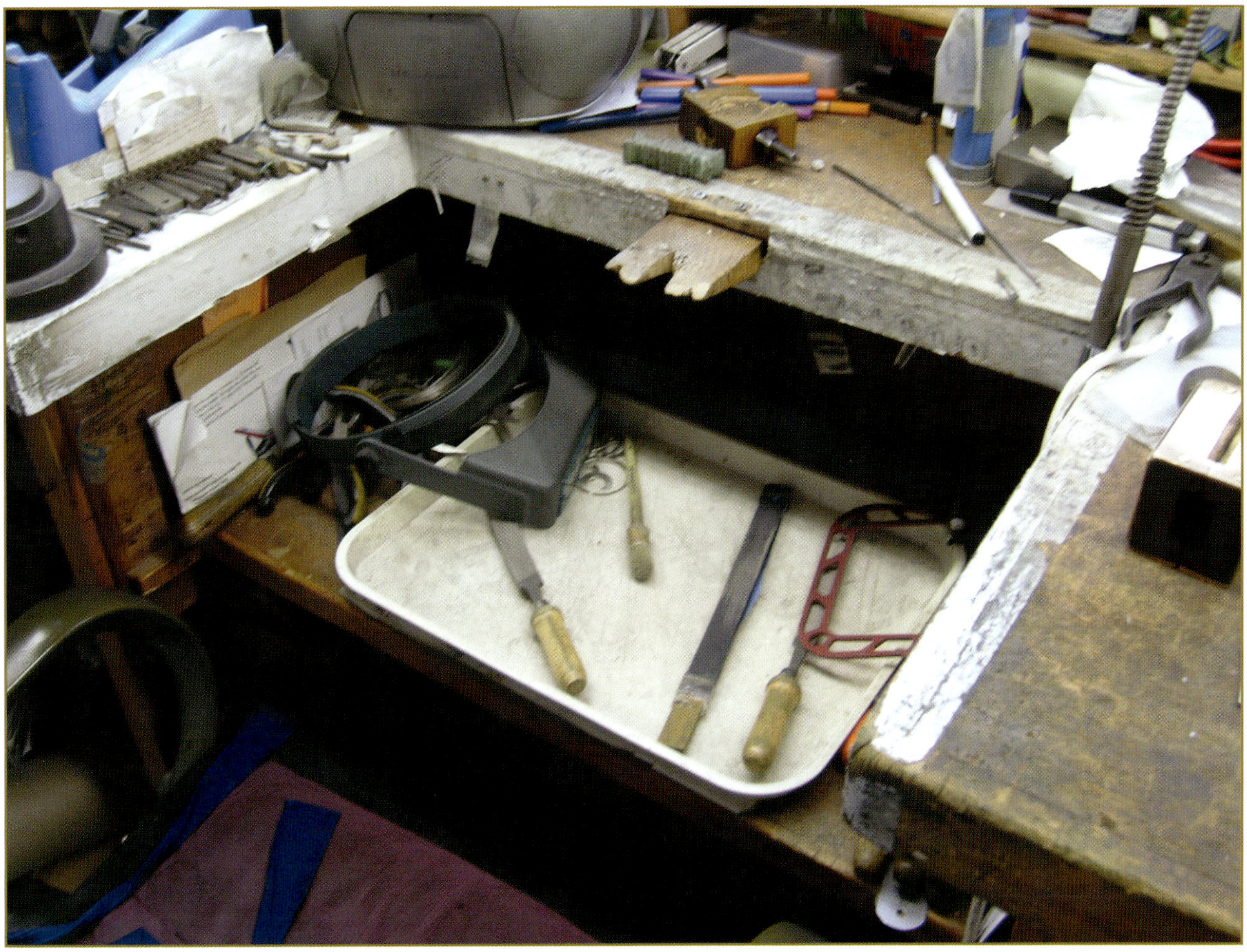

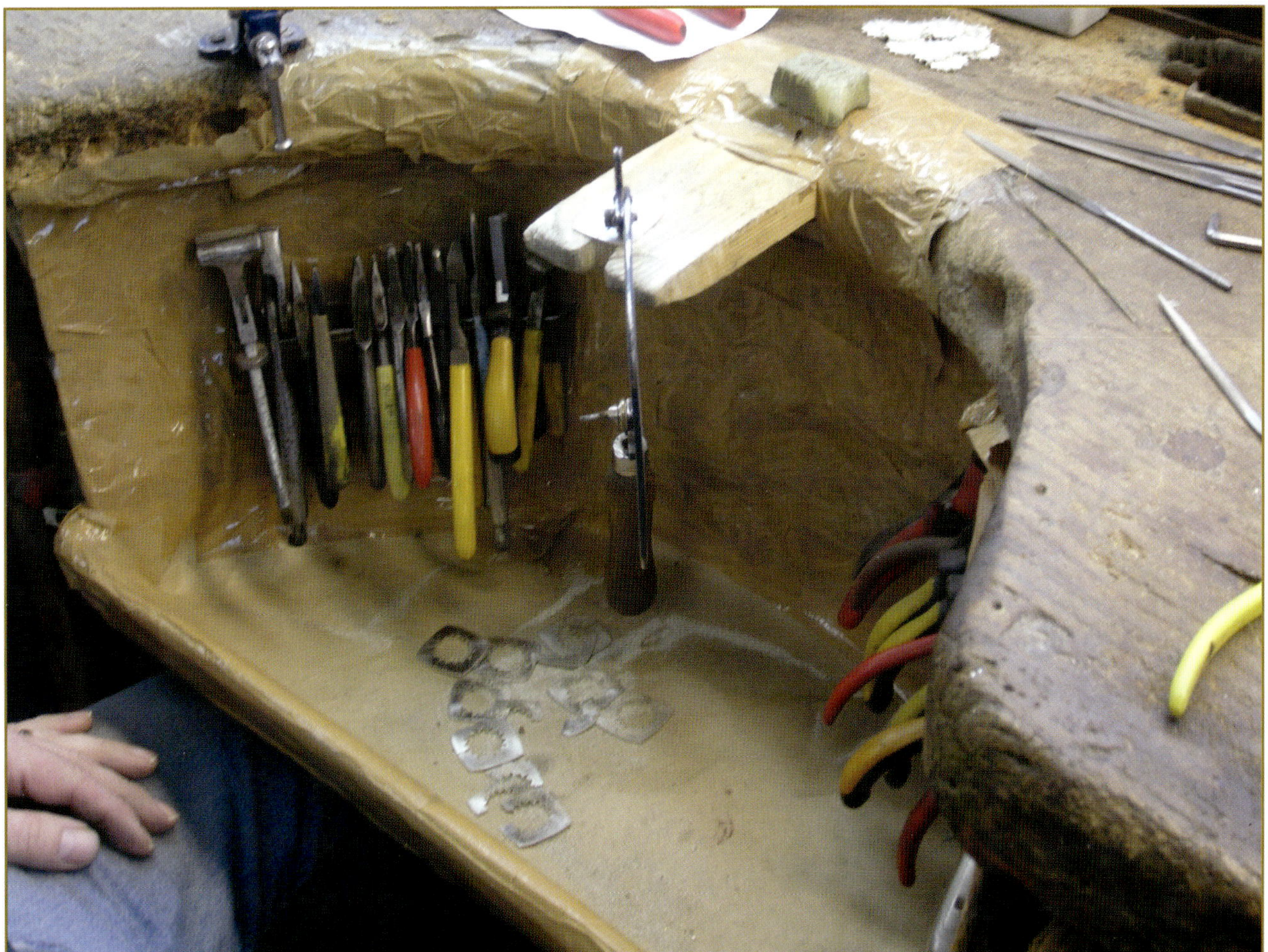

"At that time any hint of 'cyanide poisoning' required the immediate administration of Cyanide Antidote Solutions 1 and 2, sodium nitrite and sodium thiosulphate solutions, these mixed "in vitro" to form a ferric gelatinous 'gloop' that then hopefully reacted with the cyanide in the stomach. They had to be drunk by the unfortunate person, whilst he was gotten to fresh air. This was supported by a good whiff of amyl nitrite."

"Usually one good mouthful induced immediate vomiting, but, urged on by his mates, the whole measure had to be drunk…. many said it would have been better the quick death than the slow recovery. It was "kill or cure" or on occasion possibly both!"

Working at Livery Street

Much of the following information has been sourced from employees who worked at Livery Street and some of whom are still employed by W H Darby who encompass the Vaughtons brand.

Most of the tools for Vaughtons as used at Livery Street would still be in use at Well Street today, albeit in slightly modified form.

As mass production of coins and medals was accelerated towards the end of the 19th century, machines were developed to accommodate the market.

The photograph left shows one of Vaughton's Medal Copying and Reducing Lathe; it is electric powered and was designed by the Paris mechanic, V Janvier. The machine reproduced dies in various sizes. Janvier's machine could reproduce every detail of the original artist's design. This machine started at Livery Street in 1908. It can be viewed at the Thinktank Trust's Museum Collection Centre.

Right, is another machine retained at the Well Street premises of W H Darby, transferred there from the Livery Street premises and still in use till recently. This machine can exert a force of 360 tonnes and is one of the "stars" of the recently produced W H Darby CD.

It's larger cousin, known as "Big Bertha" remains in use in a local company which is adjacent to the old livery Street premises and is used for pressings, some of which include the leapers used for Jaguar Cars.

Above is a photograph of enamelling being finalised and readied for inspection; typically medals are produced by the hundred, laid out on flat trays and then visually inspected; any medal evidently "not quite right" is then rejected outright and has to be completely replaced.

The photograph below shows one of the current lathes uses for turning metal parts, note the small "furnace used to heat metal to working temperatures. Top right are some of the thousands of small tools and dies used to strike medals from.

The following two photographs on page 48 show the "sophisticated" storage methods used for nearly 200 years, note the sag imparted to the shelves through use and weighting and the implicit use of 6 inch nails to maintain them in situ.

This die store hold over 1000 dies (male and female) all organised. Held on these shelves are dies relating to FA Cup Winners, the Isle of Man TT races, Wimbledon Tennis, Cricketing, the Titanic Survivors medals as well as everyday medals from "Prefect" to "Milk Monitor".

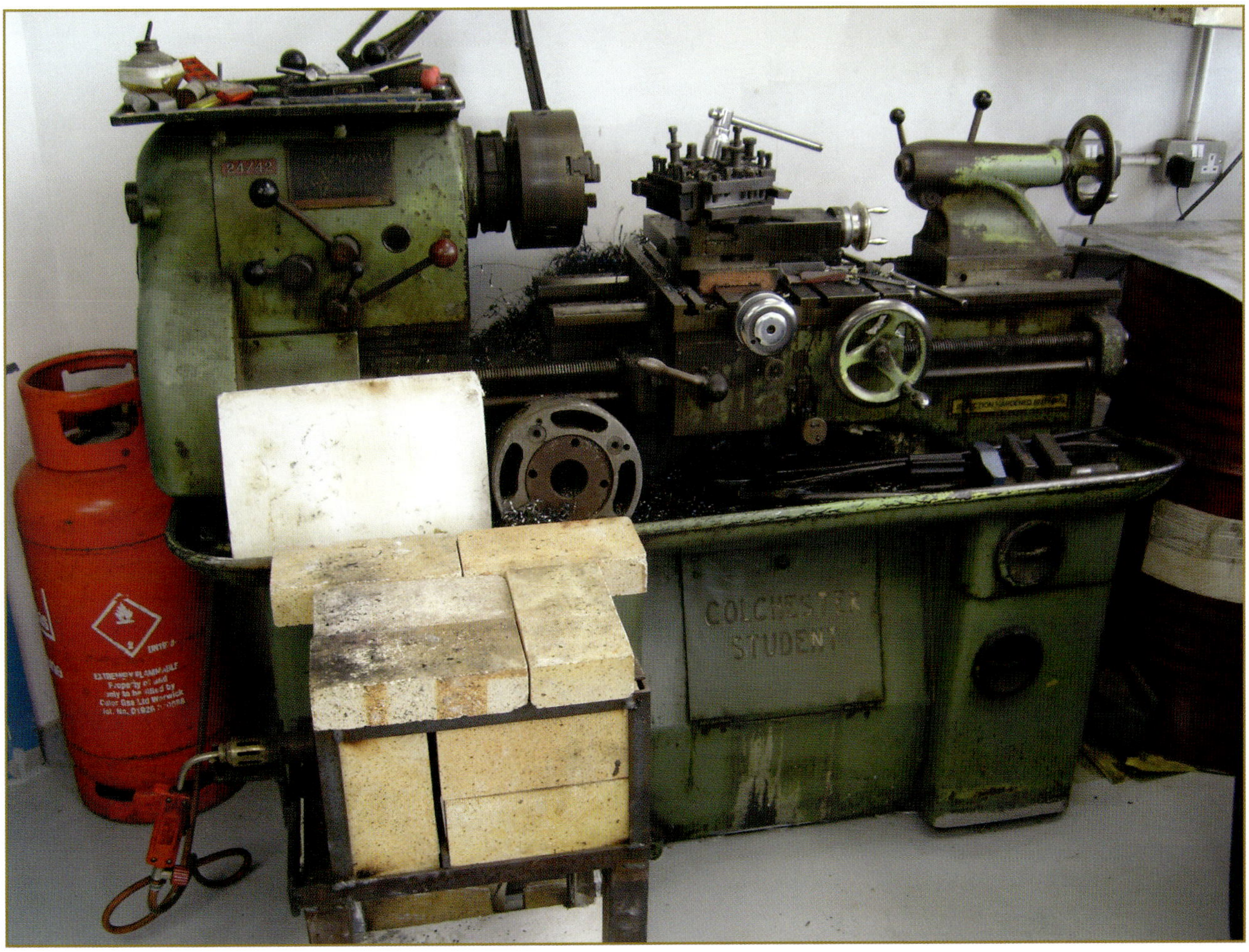

Institutes such as the Electrical Engineers, Rotary Clubs and Funeral Directors are all maintained here along with medals for the many regiments of UK and Colonial Regiments, overseas forces and specialists including the SAS.

Many of these dies include Masonic jewels including Grand Lodge and Scottish Rite. The following photograph shows in more detail the die identification; stamped into both halves of the die.

shock drive process required to obtain the most highly detailed medals requires a very robust tool. Medals may be struck individually, in small sets or by the hundred, each medal having to look identical in every respect.

The photograph below shows the modern racking system employed at the Company; much more space efficient but again showing the sheer numbers of dies and tools that are in everyday usage, each being numbered or annotated with the die it contains, each tool contains two dies.

The photograph below shows a sample of the tools used in the medal making process. Note the substantial nature of the steel dies need to withstand the pressure generated when the dies are stamped using the pressing process. Some presses are to 360 tonnes capability and the

The photograph below shows one of the guillotines used on site, this for the cutting and shearing of metal plate or strip. Despite its considerable age the piece of equipment is readily maintained and in use on a daily basis. Metal is fed in from the front of the machine and then passed through the guillotine to an adjustable backplate. The backplate is adjusted so that when the shear blade is manually operated, the correct metal size sheet is produced. His exacting measurement may require several minor adjustment to correctly size

the produced metal blank. This is done using two large bolts and spanners, this to achieve accuracy of 1/16th. of an inch.

The original guillotines were fitted without modern day guarding and the loss of a finger tip was not unknown. Guillotines were used to shear steel, brass, bronze, tin and even aluminium plate, the blank produced then being transported to and processed through dedicated Press Lines. Hundreds of medal blanks were produced this way. It was an art to maximise the number of blanks that could be produced from a single sheet of metal. Today there are computer driven machines using dedicated programmes but when the machine was first used this was calculated by hand.

Operators could be men or women and on large production runs an 8 hour working day was not uncommon, the guillotines could be hand or foot operated, either pressing a foot pedal or pulling a lever, both required considerable strength to impact the force required to shear the metal. It was not uncommon either for operators to develop musculature more heavily developed on the lever side of their body. As many guillotines and hand presses rotated clockwise, it was normally the right arm or leg that was used most frequently and accordingly, the operators right side had more strength and bulk. This was exacerbated by the practice of "piece work" where workers were paid by the piece or pieces per hour, the faster you worked the more pieces were produced, and consequently the more you got paid. Folk lore says that Birmingham women had the strongest right arms in Britain and that many a man lost an arm wrestling match to a Brummie "wench".

The following photographs show the payment records of the workers, these books are still maintained in archive at the Well Street premises and date from around 1850. All of payments are written in ink, by hand and show how few employees there were at the time

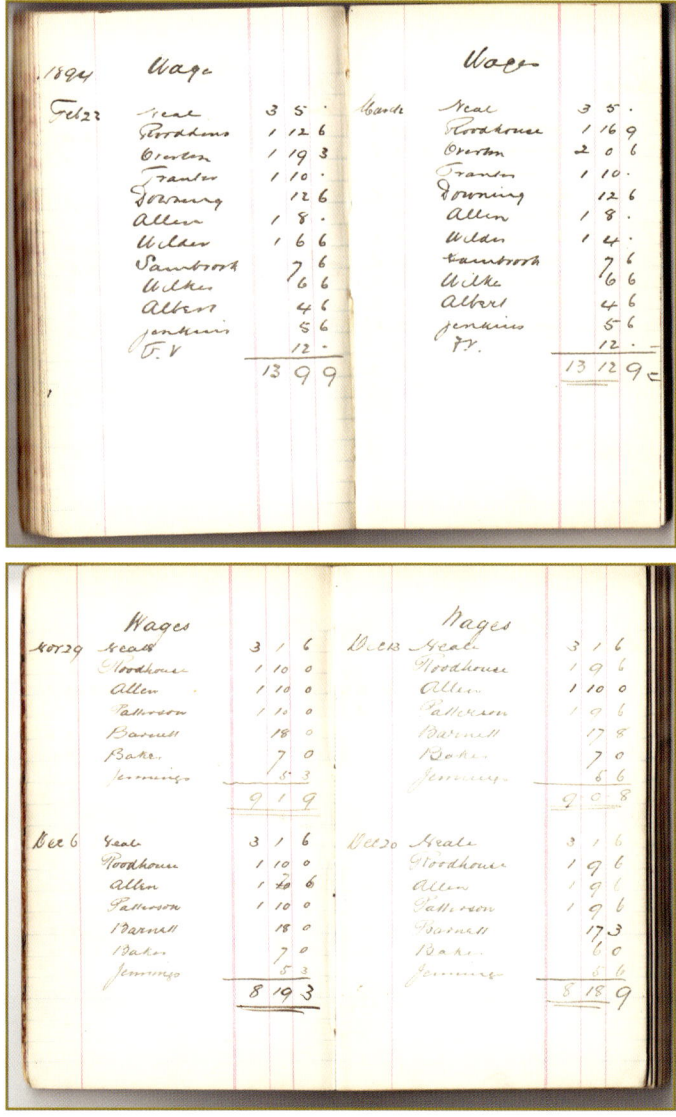

CHAPTER SIX –
OLIVER HOWARD VAUGHTON

Grandson of the founding Philip Vaughton was Oliver Howard Vaughton, born on September 1st 1861 in Aston.

"Howard" was a very famous footballer of his time, he played local football before he joined Aston Villa in August 1880 as a forward, before the Football League was formed, and played between 1880 and 1888. The team's 1880–81 season was noted as Villa having played 25 games and won 21, they also won the Staffordshire Cup that same year. He was part of the Aston Villa FA Cup winning team of 1887.

The team that day was Coulton, Warner, Dawson, Simmonds, Allen, Davis, Brown, Hunter, Vaughton, Hodgetts, Yates and Burdon.

He played in 26 FA Cup matches, scoring 15 goals. Howard was Villa's first senior international, playing five times for England and scoring six goals. Five of those came in a 13–0 victory over Ireland in Belfast in 1882.

His Villa team mate Arthur Brown scored 4 in the same match. Howard shares the record as the most goals scored by any one player in any England International game. He played his last international game for England on March 17th 1884

The following commentary of the time, abstracted from the Villa News and Record Sept 1906, summarises Vaughton's football career.

"The peoples favourite, and one of Archie Hunter's pet pupils. An adept at every form of indoor and outdoor sport, he dribbled like an angel and shot like a demon. Not nearly so deadly as his comrade, Whateley, he scored his share of goals. Whatever he did he did well, and was neatness personified. Could scarcely be played in the wrong position, and was saturated through with the Aston Villa spirit. Scored the only goal in the famous cup tie against Queens Park Rangers in Glasgow, in 1884. Made a famous wing company with Eli Davis. A keen judge of most games, a thorough sportsman, he has enriched sport in many directions".

An injury in 1888 forced him to leave football. It was after his football career ended that he came back into silversmithing to run the family firm.

He became a president of Aston Villa in 1924 and remained as a director of the club until 1932.

As a sportsman he was also a British skating champion, taking the All–England title, and played for Warwickshire, Staffordshire and Shropshire at cricket and was a county hockey player. He was also a racing cyclist and first class swimmer.

He died in January 1937.

CHAPTER SEVEN –
ASTON VILLA & THE F.A. CUP

At the Vaughton's Gothic Works, there are two coloured class windows, still there today with iconic stylised footballs, a tribute to Oliver Howard Vaughton. His picture and that of the F A Cup winning Aston Villa team still adorn the walls of the Managing Director's Office of W H Darby at their Well Street premises.

The hostel premises which now occupies the Gothic Works also has the same pictures on the wall along with a placard declaring itself as the "Home of the F A Cup". Of the four FA cups produced, Vaughtons made one of these. It was in 1895 that Vaughtons were commissioned to make a new trophy after the "old" one had been stolen from a William Shillcocks' Shoe Shop window. The thief later admitted that it had been melted down and used in coin counterfeiting. The cup was used from 1896 till 1910 when a larger trophy was then obtained by the FA.

The 2nd FA Cup

Anyone who visits the Gothic Street Works will see a placard that announces it as the "Home of the FA Cup". This should, more accurately, read "Home of the 1895 and second FA Cup.

The first FA Cup was known as the "Little Tin Idol" and it was used from 1872–1895. The name refereed to the footballer mounted atop the twin handles trophy. It was made by Martin, Hall & Co, Sheffield, and was approximately 18 inches high and cost £20.00. Infamously it was stolen from William Shillcock Outfitters Shop, being on local display in Newtown Row, Birmingham, having been won that year by Aston Villa, and despite the reward of £10, was never recovered.

Accordingly the FA "fined" Aston Villa £25 to pay for the replacement.

It was some 60 years after the theft that the thief admitted his crime, the cup being melted down and turned into counterfeit coinage as half crowns.

Vaughtons were commissioned in 1895 to make the replacement, much in the same style as the first cup, which they did. This cup was first won by The Wednesday (later to become Sheffield Wednesday) when the beat Wolverhampton Wanderers 2 -1. The game was played at Crystal Palace on April 18th.1896 in front of a crowd of 48, 836.

This cup was used until 1910 when it was found that the design had been copied; the cup was withdrawn and then presented to Lord Kinnaird for his 21 years of service as FA President. This cup was sold at Christie's on the 19th. May 2005 at £420,000 (£478,000 with fees) and acquired by David Gold, at the time, Joint Chairman of Birmingham City Football Club.

Lord Kinnaird won the FA Cup a record 5 times, three times with "Wanderers" and twice with "Old Etonians"… he also recorded the first FA Cup "own goal.

The cup can be seen at the National Football Association Museum where it is displayed on loan.

Visitors to the Gothic Works will see a series of stained glass windows; these reflect the FA cup's manufacture at the site. This "second" cup could be reconstructed as W. H Darby still have the original designs and moulds.

The 1896 Cup Final is esconsced in "lore" as follows; during the game a shot from Wednesday's Fred Spiksley, rebounded off the crossbar and hit the Wolverhampton goalkeeper, Billy Tennant, on the head so powerfully that he remained slightly concussed throughout the game which he insisted on completing. At full time he asked one of the Wednesday players, Jack Earp (captain) when the replay was… he had no recollection of any second goal… .

Wednesday's Rob (Bob) Petrie' Winners Medal from that Final was auctioned recently. The medal, as Lot 411, was sold for £10,250 including premium on October 5th. 2011.

CHAPTER EIGHT –
GRACE VAUGHTON (1905–1979)
& BRIAN VAUGHTON

Grace Vaughton

Grace Vaughton did not enter the family business directly however she was as much a professional as any male member of the lineage. She worked in the Orthoptic Department of Nottingham and Midlands Eye Infirmary and was an acknowledged expert in eye problems.

She was published in the British Journal of Opthalmology during the late 1940's and early 50's. Her paper on Hypermetropia and Squint Correction, compiled in conjunction with Maureen Stuart, assessed the identification of the underlying problem at the earliest opportunity to afford the highest chance of surgical correction.

Brian Vaughton

Brian Vaughton spent 18 years working in the family firm before leaving to pursue another career. He was an accredited MOD correspondent, mainly for aviation magazines and his articles included Wellington, Lancaster, Lightning and other period aircraft.

He had an interest in early radio (1940'-1950's). He managed to access the studio control rooms of live broadcasts of Rae Jenkins and The Midland Light Orchestra and others. Brian maintained the "creative" urge and undertook freelance journalistic work for the Birmingham Post and Birmingham Weekly Post but the BBC always beckoned.

In the 1961 and 1962 he compiled and wrote two radio programs. Both were produced by Charles Parker from BBC Birmingham studios. These were described as "The Birmingham Ballads" and went by the names of "The Jewellery" and "The Cry From The Cut".

His work encompassed;

1948   "The King of Goats" a Children's Hour Play Adaptation

1959/60 "Moments of Truth"

1963   "The Cat's Whiskers" 40th. Anniversary of Broadcasting in the Midlands.

1963/4 "A Girls Best Friend" 2 programmes

1969   "They Brought The Sea to Manchester" … the 75th. Anniversary of the Manchester Ship Canal.

There are many others.

"The Jewellery" was an actual radio ballad on the Birmingham Jewellery Quarter and was based on his experiences within Vaughtons. It was homage to what he felt was a passing lifestyle before it was lost forever. He recalled that many craftsmen were tempted by the promise of higher wages offered by the Austin Motor Company, Longbridge. As craftsmen left to become carmakers they became impossible to replace in the Quarter.

Mass production on an industrial scale pervaded the jewellery industry, which he felt, meant that standards were getting lower and the desire for speed and output killed the trade. Indeed, to stress the point, in regard to his own business (Vaughtons) he made reference to a quotation attributed to John Ruskin; *"There is scarcely anything in the world that some man cannot make a little worse, and sell a little more cheaply. The person who buys on price alone is this man's lawful prey"*.

Taken from *"The Jewellery"*, his own script, comes the following….

> *Today I'll wear a diamond clear*
> *Tomorrow perhaps a pearl*
> *Or emerald green or ruby red*
> *All stones to thrill a girl*
> *It can be hard to choose the kind*
> *Topaz, or sapphire blue*
> *And even then 'Ill change my mind*
> *As any girl can do…*
> *Life never changes…*

CHAPTER NINE – ADVERTISING

One of the more difficult tasks undertaken in producing this volume was in obtaining Vaughtons advertising. Vaughtons appear to have produced only limited advertising, usually in very plain styles and then only to support specific areas of production or even at a specific exhibition. The following examples show how these were produced.

The first advert is detailed as being from 1891 however it shows the company being at Gothic Works which happened after this date. The masonic medal is displayed alongside a button.

The advert below is some 20 years later and shows the Wolverhampton Automobile Club badge, the advert emphasising Cycle name plates.

The nature of the adverts was always very plain, simple and the graphics very direct and to the point. Function over form was clearly the ethic of the day. For a company producing some of the most elegant, complex and sophisticated designs ever produced in medals, badges and localosities this contradiction appears to have been cash driven. Medals were produced from the highest quality materials available and this left little for the adverts. As such the marketing of Vaughtons was more through the exceptional pieces produced rather than costly adverts.

This advert shows the Southampton County Motor Club and incorporates an automotive link with the upper engine cylinder design.

The photo below shows a complete change in font style and uses Vaughtons Ltd rather than the plain Vaughtons business name.

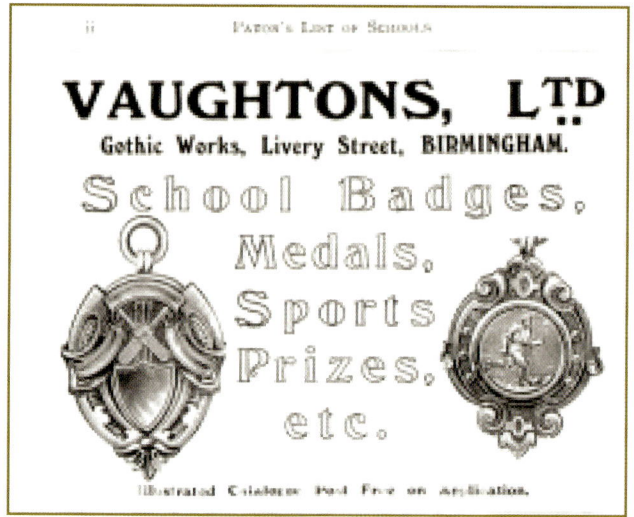

This all changes around 1902 when the following catalogue was produced. It shows a much more elegant house style, incorporating masonic emblems in profusion. The Vaughtons Trade Mark is also shown. This Eighth Edition shows the square and compass, trowel, sceptre, maul and sword and two six pointed stars comprised of two interwoven triangles. The cover declares there to be two telephone lines, Central 3430 and 3431. The company is also to be contacted via Telegram at Emblems, Birmingham.

The catalogue is comprised of the most highly detailed photographs of all of the regalia and medals produced by the company and was also designed in house. This catalogue forms part of the current collection maintained and displayed at Well Street.

Many of the photographs shown in the next chapter come directly from this volume.

CHAPTER TEN –
VAUGHTONS & FREEMASONRY

For those who have seen 92 Livery Street, the 'Gothic Works' designed by Sidney H Vaughton, its 'free Jacobean' style frontage is both elegant and eloquent. The elegance of its design shown in the terra cotta wording, some of which has been broken away, shows the importance of the building to its owner, Philip Vaughton and his sons. Its eloquence is in its design components that encompass several, clearly intended Masonic iconographic elements.

The lower floor windows show a central 'key stone' element often seen in Royal Arch masonry. This keystone design is also used in elements of the company's Royal Arch jewel designs. The central windows show a symmetry of three, again a key number in the Royal Arch, these being allied to the elevation consistent with free Jacobean architectural form.

The building's central front-end gable is topped by a 'Masonic square', a tool used by stonemasons to check angles in worked stone and buildings and adopted into freemasonry within its 'working tools'. It has two Masonically significant pillars (representations of the porchway or entrance to King Solomon's Temple), these being topped by further Masonic icons. A further Masonic element shows a 'third, central pillar' reaching to the roof apex touching the centre of the angle of the square. This is an allegorical illusion to a connection with the 'all seeing eye'.

The whole frontage appears to give a very clear indication that Sidney Vaughton, architect and possible practitioner to the 'Great Architect of the Universe', was leaving to history a very clear and concise message for those open to its interpretation.

The original engraving of the building shows that a sturdy flagpole topped the building and it is shown very clearly flying the union flag.

In respect of John Vaughton's recent recollections *"Although I am not a mason myself, I do know that there is a considerable demand for supplying Masonic Lodges with both jewellery and other regalia, such as aprons, collars, gauntlets and rings. During my time with Vaughtons Ltd we had an office in Bradford. It was run by a Freemason who specialised in obtaining orders from Masonic Lodges for their jewellery requirements. And in Gothic Works we concentrated on making the gold jewellery ordered, such as the Square and Compass, which has been called 'the most significant symbol in Masonry".*

Medals, Badges, **Cups, Shields, &c.**

1209 S
Wreath and Shield. Stock reverse
in various sizes.

211
"SCIENCE," by Albert Toft

4001 X
Cup.

A24
Military Medal.

VI.
Coronation Medal
(Modelled by Frank Bowcher.)
Samples and prices on
application.

264
Committee Badges.
Any other officer's title may be substituted.
Enamelled.

AO 1
Saw-pierced and
Engraved Ribbon,
Gold Wreath.

VS6   **VS8**   **VS7**

180b
School Badge.
(Cost of Die, 55/-)

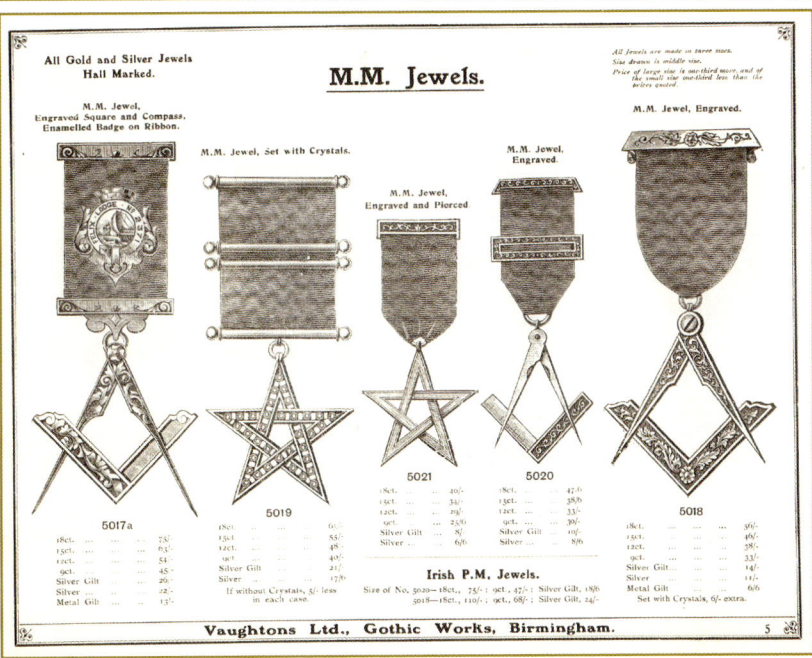

All Gold and Silver Jewels
Hall Marked.

M.M. Jewels.

All Jewels are made in three sizes.
Size drawn is middle size.
Price of large size is one-third more, and of
the small size one-third less than the
prices quoted.

M.M. Jewel,
Engraved Square and Compass.
Enamelled Badge on Ribbon.

M.M. Jewel, Set with Crystals.

M.M. Jewel,
Engraved and Pierced.

M.M. Jewel,
Engraved.

M.M. Jewel, Engraved.

5017a   **5019**   **5021**   **5020**   **5018**

Irish P.M. Jewels.

All Gold and Silver Jewels
Hall Marked.

Provincial Grand Lodge Jewels,
and "London Rank."

All Jewels are made in three sizes.
Size drawn is middle size.
Price of large size is one-third more, and of
the small size one-third less than the
prices quoted.

Past Provincial Officer's Jewel.

Provincial Officer's Collar Jewel
(Star and Triangle on Chaplain's Jewel only,
emblems alone on others.)

Past Provincial Officer's
Jewel.

5056a
Emblem on Blue Enamelled Oval.

5056b
Emblem on Blue Enamelled Oval.

5055

5056
Emblem on Blue Enamelled Oval.

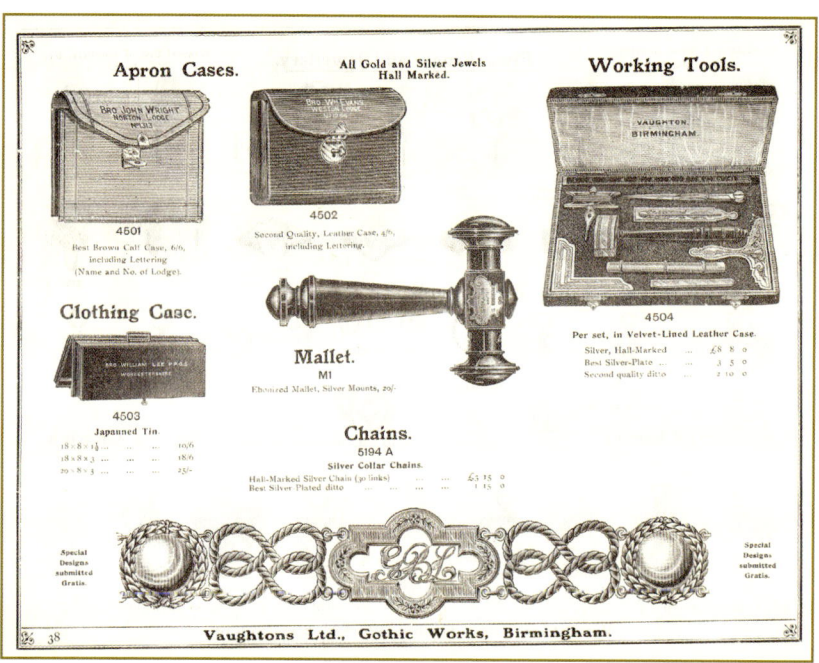

Apron Cases.

All Gold and Silver Jewels Hall Marked.

Working Tools.

4501
Best Brown Calf Case, 6/6, including Lettering (Name and No. of Lodge).

4502
Second Quality, Leather Case, 4/6, including Lettering.

Clothing Case.

4503
Japanned Tin.

18 × 8 × 1½ 16/6
18 × 8 × 3 ... ... 18/6
20 × 8 × 3 ... ... 25/-

Mallet.

M1
Ebonised Mallet, Silver Mounts, 20/-

Chains.

5194 A
Silver Collar Chains.
Hall-Marked Silver Chain (30 links) ... £3 15 0
Best Silver Plated ditto 1 15 0

4504
Per set, in Velvet-Lined Leather Case.
Silver, Hall-Marked £8 8 0
Best Silver-Plate 3 5 0
Second quality ditto 2 10 0

Special Designs submitted Gratis.

Special Designs submitted Gratis.

Vaughtons Ltd., Gothic Works, Birmingham.

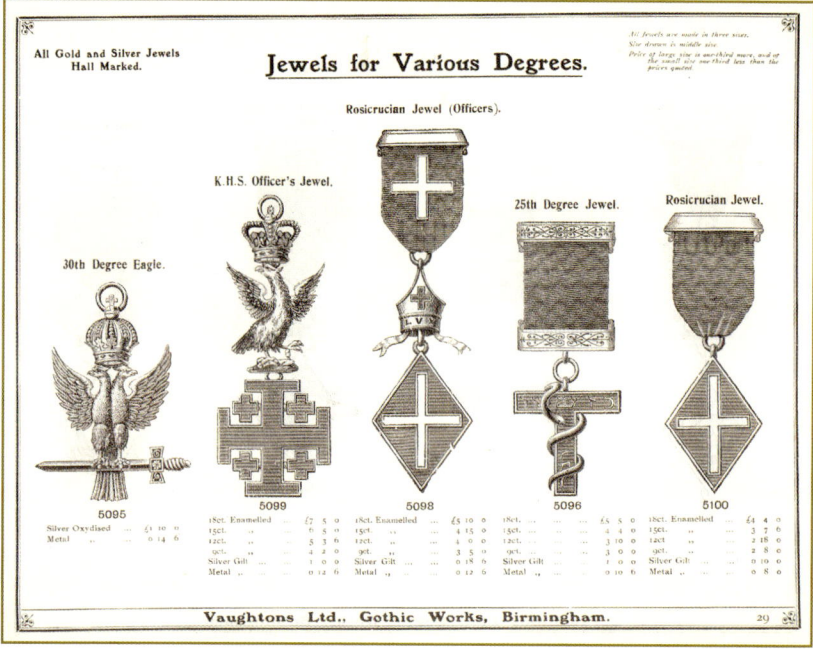

Jewels for Various Degrees.

All Gold and Silver Jewels Hall Marked.

All Jewels are made in three sizes. Size drawn is middle size. Price of large size is one-third more, and of the small size one-third less than the prices quoted.

Rosicrucian Jewel (Officers).

K.H.S. Officer's Jewel.

25th Degree Jewel.

Rosicrucian Jewel.

30th Degree Eagle.

5095
Silver Oxydised ... £1 10 0
Metal 0 14 6

5099
18ct. Enamelled ... £7 5 0
15ct. ... 5 8 0
12ct. ... 5 3 6
9ct. ... 4 2 0
Silver Gilt ... 1 0 0
Metal ... 0 12 6

5098
18ct. Enamelled ... £5 10 0
15ct. ... 4 15 0
12ct. ... 4 0 0
9ct. ... 3 5 0
Silver Gilt ... 0 18 0
Metal ... 0 12 6

5096
18ct. Enamelled ... £5 5 0
15ct. ... 4 4 0
12ct. ... 3 10 0
9ct. ... 3 0 0
Silver Gilt ... 0 18 0
Metal ... 0 10 0

5100
18ct. Enamelled ... £4 4 0
15ct. ... 3 7 6
12ct. ... 2 18 0
9ct. ... 2 8 0
Silver Gilt ... 0 10 0
Metal ... 0 8 0

Vaughtons Ltd., Gothic Works, Birmingham.

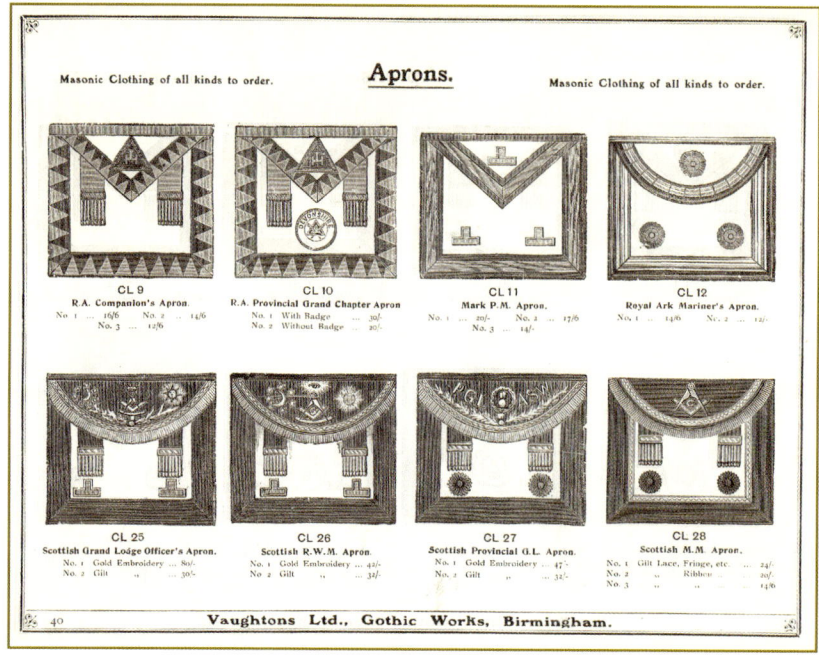

Aprons.

Masonic Clothing of all kinds to order.

Masonic Clothing of all kinds to order.

CL 9
R.A. Companion's Apron.
No. 1 ... 16/6   No. 2 ... 14/6
No. 3 ... 12/6

CL 10
R.A. Provincial Grand Chapter Apron.
No. 1 With Badge ... 36/-
No. 2 Without Badge ... 30/-

CL 11
Mark P.M. Apron.
No. 1 ... 20/-   No. 2 ... 17/6
No. 3 ... 14/-

CL 12
Royal Ark Mariner's Apron.
No. 1 ... 14/6   No. 2 ... 12/-

CL 25
Scottish Grand Lodge Officer's Apron.
No. 1 Gold Embroidery ... 80/-
No. 2 Gilt 30/-

CL 26
Scottish R.W.M. Apron.
No. 1 Gold Embroidery ... 42/-
No. 2 Gilt 32/-

CL 27
Scottish Provincial G.L. Apron.
No. 1 Gold Embroidery ... 47/-
No. 2 Gilt 32/-

CL 28
Scottish M.M. Apron.
No. 1 Gilt Lace, Fringe, etc. ... 24/-
No. 2 Ribbon ... 20/-
No. 3 ... 14/6

Vaughtons Ltd., Gothic Works, Birmingham.

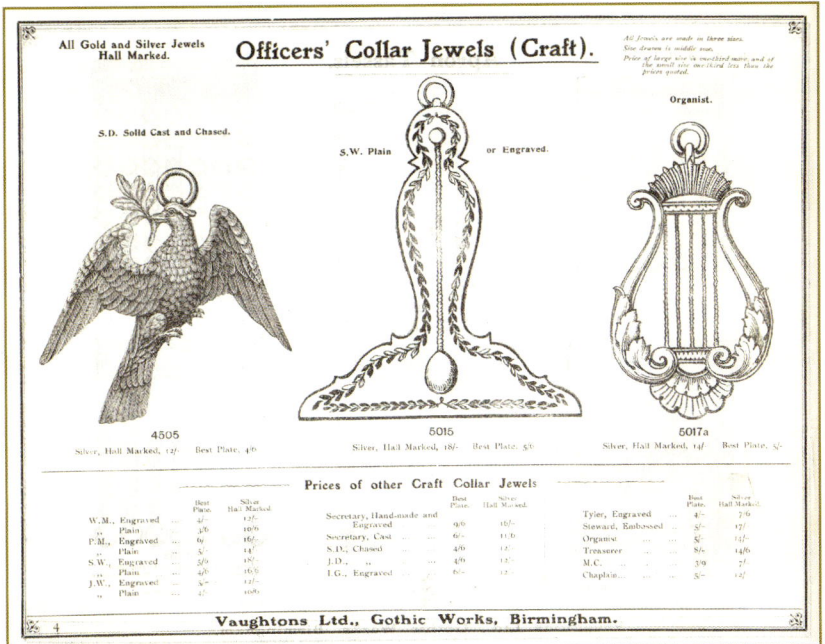

Indeed this Masonic connection with Bradford has been confirmed by one single advertising plate and medal cases (not however medals) inscribed with typically 'Medallist Badgemakers', Vaughtons Birmingham, Bradford and London.

From recent Masonic searches made two Vaughton individuals have been confirmed as Masons but no others to date.

Thomas Vaughton
Elkington Lodge No 1016, Birmingham
Initiated: 23rd March 1865, Passed: 27th April 1865, Raised: 25th May 1865
Address: Lozells   Occupation: jeweller
Master of the lodge in 1873 and made an Honorary Member in 1886
Holte Lodge No 1246, Aston
One of the founders of this lodge in 1868 he was Master in 1872 and made an Honorary Member in 1885

Oliver Vaughton
Elkington Lodge No 1016, Birmingham
Initiated: 23rd March 1865, Passed: 27th April 1865, Raised: 25th May 1865
Address: Lozells   Occupation: Jeweller
Master of the lodge in 1870 and resigned in September 1886

In compiling 'Vaughton's' archive some 200 job cards showing all types of Masonic jewels have been collated, indexed and scanned. These cards show the workings from a simple pencil or inked sketch, to addition of colour wash or chroma wash, with all detail and inscription. In some cases the original medal, or augmentation components of the medal has been found attached.

Certain societies had special themes and one such item within the Vaughton Archive shows a Burns Night celebration where the front cover was transposed to the Chair's Masters Chain of Office .

The two photographs above are a single piece hand painted onto cardboard and typical of the graphics of the period. The left hand side image is a jewel to be agreed upon before production for the Lodge of St Michael No.4426. The left hand side image shows the detail of the centrepiece which shows Saint Michael with sword and shield backed by the square and compass. Thousands of such pieces passed through for approval and the customer would annotate these images before the final design was made.

The pendant square could be ordered in over 50 different styles, the "Euclidian" (to us Pythagorus Square) was similarly available. Pendant squares typically were engraved on their reverse with the recipients name, office, year in office and the gratitude of the brethren. Some squares were "hinged" back to back so the father and son could be added. Two examples exist in the Vaughton Archive of "triple hinged" squares were grandfather, father, son and grandson to be have space allocated to celebrate the continuity of fraternity.

The placement of a single diamond on the Euclidyan was recorded in the following workbooks for two masons on the achievement of 50 years service to the Craft

In researching this book over 900 such pieces were recovered. Some 200 such pieces were dated, preserved and displayed in recent exhibitions including Grand Lodge in London.

The photograph top left hand of page 61 shows another such "job card" reference D1828, this being a Founder Jewel for Martello Lodge No. 8712. This shows an Agreed Job, as indicated by the rather more impressive backing card. This is how the customer would have been presented with a "final approval". The customer having signed and dated his approval, the jewel would have then gone to the Production Department.

Hundreds of job sheets were kept on site, some 3 boxes of "English Biscuits" contained elements of over many, many designs and redrafts, most initially drawn in pencil or pen, pasted from books, annotated with wording and colour suggestions. Pasting was a favourite method of setting out a typical base design. This was then "worked up" to the customer's requirements. A coloured design

Taillandiers were located at 41 Tenby Street North, Birmingham. Their price list ranges from 4/6d per pound to 20s per pound and each also displays a cost per ounce. Camel hair shading brushes were 4 shillings per dozen. "Ideal Essence" Fat and Semi Fat was highlighted as "the best vehicle for enamel painting" at 2/3d and 2/6d respectively as supplied in half ounce bottles… .

Also supplied were cutting edge products at the time, Translucid and Extra Soft Translucid Enamels, reflecting their cost in the process are quoted at 16 shillings per ounce.

Also available for supplier were gold, silver and platinum leaf (for Paillonner) in 4 inch squares, gold was advertised at 2/6d per sheet and silver at 8d.

The costs of these consumables reflected the exception standards of Vaughton's goods.

Certain lodges procured there entire set of Lodge Offices jewels in boxed sets although very few of this are now complete today. Records show how gold pieces were put together and even today the manner of their construction is remarkable. Certain jewels involved soldering of small components which was simple enough, however

would then be established. These had the in house name of "chroma". Chromas were hand painted, shaded, tinted, highlighted and given a three dimensional appearance to show the designs of to their best advantage.

Customers could choose from perhaps 20 shades of gold and similarly silver, have specific patinas as required, select from hundreds of ribbon colours and any number of adornments and additions. You "paid your money and yer takes yer choice…".

The 1929 P Taillander & Son, Enamel and Colour Manufacturers and Dealers Catalogue, again held in the Vaughton's Archive lists many enamels used at the time….Amethyst, Azure, Crimson, Carmine Nos. 1 and 2, Paillons Dark, Medium and Light, Electric, Moonlight, Lavender, Llibellula, Peackock, Primrose, gentian, Flag, Celestial, Heliotrope, Hortensa, Imperial, Lavidia, Lapis Nos. 1–4, Memphis, Pompadour, Thetis, Saffire, Semiramis, Titania, Velvet Copper and holds listings of complete sections for "Blues", "Greens", and all manner of colours.

Rose enamels came in shades of Night Nos. 1 and 2, Sweet Briar, Red Currant, Raspberry, Lightning, Vermillion, Glowing, Gladiola and Champagne.

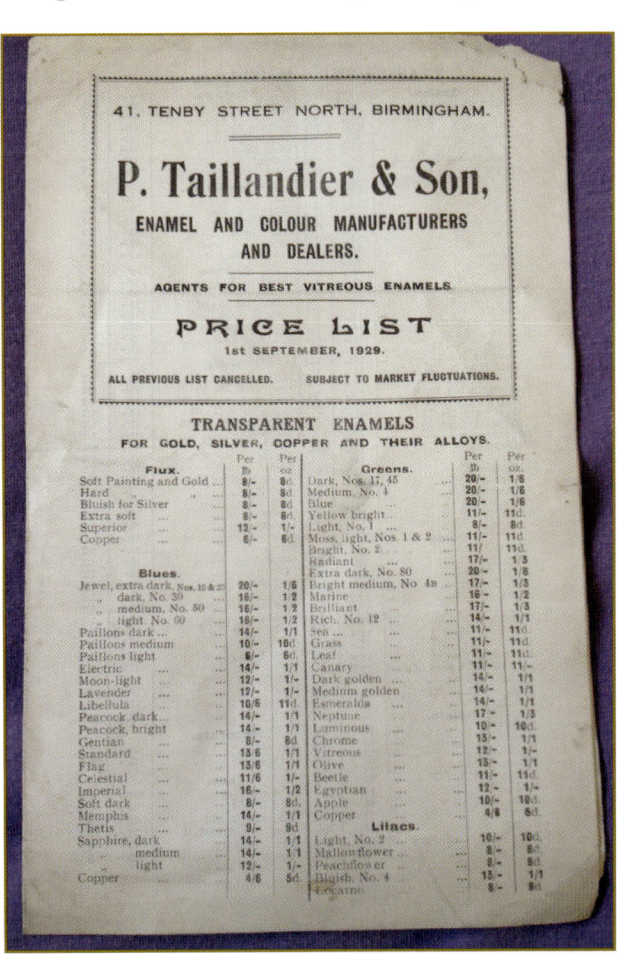

a backing piece was often added and how this was completed was almost impossible to understand until you see "blind soldering" in action… even today this process is a closely guarded secret. The zenith of such work is seen in mayoral and civic chains where the jointing work is almost truly invisible. A Vaughtons salesman's brief case still exists where a client would select the components required for his or her chain, these pieces would be initially pinned in situ, usually on a blue collar wore by the recipient. The entire, fully assembled entity would then be sent off to become a fully functioning item. This case remains in Mr. Hobbis personal collection.

Numerous jewels were supported by precious and/or semi precious stones which were designed as an implicit part of the entity. Knights Templar jewels were very often inlaid with red stones forming the typical "cross" centrepiece.

Whilst researching the VAUGHTON family it soon became apparent that there was a very strong link with Freemasonry.

First Grand Lodge

Freemasonry in the UK is recognised as having developed from the ca. 1700s. The early history of Grand Lodge remains uncertain, as no formal or recorded minutes were taken until 1723. What is apparent is that in 1716, four lodges and "some old Brothers" met at the Apple Tree Tavern in Covent Garden and agreed to meet again the next year to form a "Grand Lodge". These were the Goose and Gridiron, the Crown, the Apple Tree, and the Rummer and Grapes. The "old Brothers" were probably from the Cheshire Cheese and at least one other lodge and held an assembly at the Goose and Gridiron, in St. Paul's Churchyard, on, 24 June 1717 (the Feast of St. John the Baptist). They agreed to restore their "Quarterly Communications", four meetings a year for the transaction of masonic business, and an annual assembly to elect the next Grand Master. At this meeting, they elected Anthony Sayer, Master of

the lodge at the Apple Tree, of whom little else is known, and the Grand Lodge of London and Westminster was born. At this stage, it is unlikely that they saw themselves as anything more than an association of London lodges. This perception was to change very rapidly.

The following year, one George Payne became the Grand Master. He was a career civil servant with the commissioners of taxes. In 1719, John Theophilus Desaguliers, a clergyman, an eminent scientist, and a Fellow of the Royal Society was elected. The last commoner to serve as Grand Master was George Payne in his second term of office in 1720/21, when he wrote "The General Regulations of a Free Mason" which were later incorporated in Anderson's Constitutions. Thereafter, in what appears to be a deliberate attempt to raise the profile of the organisation, all the Grand Masters have been members of the nobility. Desaguliers is often described as the "father" of modern freemasonry.

Even in London, there were many lodges that never affiliated with the new Grand Lodge. These unaffiliated Masons and their Lodges were referred to as "Old Masons," or "St. John Masons", and "St. John Lodges". Nonetheless, the influence of the new central body spread quickly, and the 1725 minutes mention lodges in ten provincial towns as far north as Salford, with Provincial Grand Lodges in South Wales and Cheshire.

In the same year, a second Grand Lodge was founded in Ireland, which took several decades to bring all the Irish lodges under its wing. Rival Grand Lodges quickly appeared in Munster and Cork. It was in Ireland that the practice of recognising the regularity of a lodge by the issue of a warrant began, the first known example dating from 1731. The Grand Lodge of Scotland was not formed until 1736.

Vaughton's records were an invaluble source of lodge histories and listings of lodges, many of whom have long ceased, are still maintained in the Vaughtons' archive.

The following photograph has been supplied via Freemason's Hall.

CHAPTER ELEVEN – THE FUTURE

We are proud of the heritage and history of Vaughtons, and we want to embellish and enrich this going forward. Our skills, craftsmanship and quality will remain the same, however we look to continually move into different sectors, allowing the name and brand of Vaughtons to expand.

Our most recent achievement is to become 1st. tier suppliers to Aston Martin, and our goal is to move further into the Automotive field.

We want to integrate our concepts and creative thinking, driving forward to manufacture high quality jewels, automotive badges, medals and other items that forever exceed expectations.

We hope to always keep the firm as a family business, and continue the ethics and roots founded by Philip Vaughton, and maybe one day our children will continue this too… .

Nick & Danielle Hobbis

APPENDIX 1

Family Tree–Phillip Vaughton (direct line)

Direct Line

PHILLIP VAUGHTON

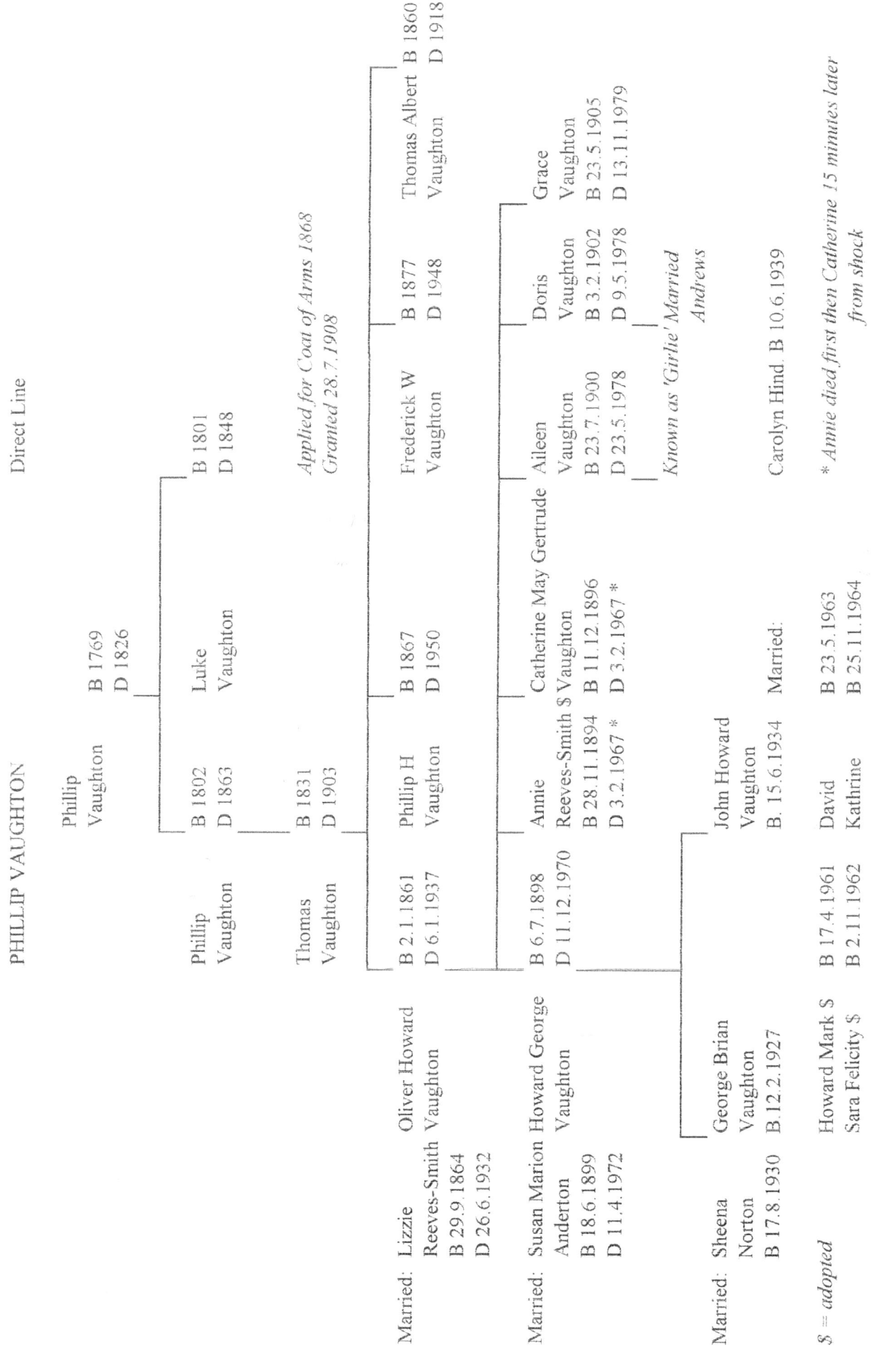

Phillip
Vaughton
B 1769
D 1826

B 1801
D 1848

Luke
Vaughton

Thomas Albert B 1860
Vaughton   D 1918

*Applied for Coat of Arms 1868
Granted 28.7.1908*

Phillip
Vaughton
B 1802
D 1863

Thomas
Vaughton
B 1831
D 1903

Phillip H
Vaughton
B 1867
D 1950

Frederick W
Vaughton
B 1877
D 1948

Grace
Vaughton
B 23.5.1905
D 13.11.1979

Married: Lizzie
Reeves-Smith
B 29.9.1864
D 26.6.1932

Oliver Howard
Vaughton
B 2.1.1861
D 6.1.1937

Catherine May Gertrude
Reeves-Smith $ Vaughton
B 11.12.1896
D 3.2.1967 *

Aileen
Vaughton
B 23.7.1900
D 23.5.1978

Doris
Vaughton
B 3.2.1902
D 9.5.1978

*Known as 'Girlie' Married
Andrews*

Married: Susan Marion
Anderton
B 18.6.1899
D 11.4.1972

Howard George
Vaughton

Annie
Reeves-Smith
B 28.11.1894
D 3.2.1967 *

John Howard
Vaughton
B. 15.6.1934

Carolyn Hind. B 10.6.1939

Married: Sheena
Norton
B 17.8.1930

George Brian
Vaughton
B.12.2.1927

Married:

B 6.7.1898
D 11.12.1970

$ = adopted

Howard Mark $
Sara Felicity $

David
Kathrine

B 23.5.1963
B 25.11.1964

B 17.4.1961
B 2.11.1962

*Annie died first then Catherine 15 minutes later
from shock*

APPENDIX 2

Family Trees, Vaughton Family

VAUGHTON FAMILY TREE

Blue indicates known jeweller

Philip Vaughton

Philip Vaughton
Baptised 27.5.1743

John Vaughton
Baptised 1.7.1748

(Marries) - Elizabeth

Luke Vaughton
Baptised 30.11.1745

Thomas Vaughton
Born 1776
(Marries) - Ann
(Born 1777)

PHILIP VAUGHTON

PHILIP
Born 1769
Baptised 23.6.1775
Died 1826

(Marries) - Mary Hares (or *Ayres*)
15.1.1797

(Marries) - Mary (born 1796)

Maria (B. 1818)

Philip Vaughton
Born 7.10.1802
Died 5.6.1863

(Marries) - Mary (born 1806)

Luke Vaughton
Born 1801
Died 1849

(Marries) - Eliza Cottrill (born 1827)

Mary (B. 1821)
Maria (B. 1826)
Phillip (B. 1826)
Elizabeth (B. 1826)
Sarah (B. 1828)
Luke (B. 1828)
Edward (B. 1832)
Emma (B. 1837)
Louisa (B. 1839)

Thomas (B. 1831)
Elizabeth (B. 1832)
Mary Ann (B. 1835)
Oliver (B. 1839)
Charles (B. 1840)

(Marries) - Rosina (born 1837)

See page 2 A

Census addresses:

1841	1 Penns Lane, Sutton
1851	127 Hampton Street
1861 & 1871	87 Lozells Road
1881	118 Heathfield Rd

46 Hospital Street

Mary Ann, Oliver & mother

PHILIP VAUGHTON FAMILY TREE

Father

PHILIP (B 1802)

	Thomas	Elizabeth	Mary Ann Rosina	Oliver	Charles
Born	1831	1832	1835	1839	1840
Married	Rosina			Clara Martin (B.1834)	
Died	1903	1841	1858	1902	

Children		Born		Born		Born		Born
	Thomas Albert	1860				Constance	1861	
	Oliver Howard	1861						
	Ernest E.	1863						
	Florence A.	1865						
	Phillip H.	1867						
	Rosina J.	1869						
	Sidney H.	1870						
	Arthur K.	1871						
	Walter S.	1873						
	Gertrude A.	1875						
	Frederick W.	1877						

See pages 3A & 3B & 3C

Census addresses:

1861	127 Hampton Street	87 Lozells Street
1871	127 Hampton Street	87 Loxells Street
1881	129 Albert Road	118 Heathfield Road
1891	94 Trinity Road	57 Guest Street
1901		(With mother & Mary Ann)

Blue indicates jeweller

69

LUKE VAUGHTON FAMILY TREE

Father

LUKE (B 1801)

	Mary	Phillip	Elizabeth	Sarah Jelico
		1826		
Born	1821	1826	1826	1828
Married		Eliza Cottrill		
Died	1871	1900	1841	1844

Children

Born   Born   Born

Census addresses:

1861	
1871	21 Vyse Street
1881	21 Vyse Street
1891	32 Barker Street

Blue indicates jeweller

LUKE VAUGHTON FAMILY TREE

Father   LUKE (B 1801)

	Luke	Edward	Emma	Louisa L.
Born	1828	1832	1837	1839
Married	Selina			
Died	1886	1895		1842

Children

	Born			Born
Kate		1853	Edward E	1857
Clara		1857	Amelia E.	1859
Susan		1859	Phillip Gilbert	1861
Luke		1861	Vincent V.	1864
Frederick		1864	Leonard H.	1865
Betty		1866	Ada Gertrude	1868
Lizzie		1868		
Thomas		1871		

See pages 3 D & E   *See page 3 F*

Census addresses:

1861	123 Well Street	195 Warstones Lane
1871	123 Well Street	47 Augusta Street
1881	25 James Street	15 Claremont Road, Handsworth
1891		32 Clarement Road, Handsworth
1901		

Blue indicates jeweller

PHILIP VAUGHTON FAMILY TREE

THOMAS (B 1831)

Father

	Thomas Albert	Oliver Howard	Ernest E.	Florence A.	Philip H.
Born	1860	2.1.1861	1863	1865	1867
Married	Clara (B 1860)	Lizzie I Reeves-Smith B 1866 D 1932	Julia Matthews (B.1870)		
Died	1918	6.1.1937			1950

			Born		**Born**
Children	Dorothy	1888 Annie Reeves-Smith		1895 Margaret	1890
		Catherine M.		1897 Tetyalan	1891
		Howard George	6.7.1898 James	1894
			1900 Dorothy	1896
		Aileen	Robert	1897
		Doris	Earnest	1899
		Grace	Tom	1900

			Hannah	
			Matthews	1842

*Coat of Arms
awarded 28.7.1908*

Census addresses:

1891	123 Lichfield Road Sutton		
1901	Anchorage Road (With Sarah Insley B.1866) (Servant in 1891!)	"Goldthorne" Ascot Road	15 Church Street Towyn	94 Trinity Rd
			Dorothy (See 3D)	

Blue indicates jeweller

72

PHILIP VAUGHTON FAMILY TREE

THOMAS (B 1831)

Father

Rosina Julia	Sidney Herbert	Arthur Rowland	Walter Septimus
1869	1870	1871	1873

Born
Married 1893 Mary Ann James (B 1873) Louisa (B. 1875) Eva (B. 1875)
Died 1949 1947 1957

Gertruda Adelaide
1875

Born Born Born Born

Children
Mildred Ida	1896
May Alice Victoria	1898
Sidney James Johno	1899
Barbara Vera	1900

Census addresses:
1901   46 Witon Road   Rectory Row   93 Grove Lane
Handsworth

Page 3B

Blue indicates jeweller

73

PHILIP VAUGHTON FAMILY TREE

THOMAS (B 1831)

Father   Frederick W.

Born   1877
Married
Died   1948

                                Born

Children

Census addresses:
1901   94 Trinity Road

Blue indicates jeweller

PHILIP VAUGHTON FAMILY TREE

Page 3D

Father   LUKE (B 1828)

	Kate	Clara	Susannah	Luke	Frederick
Born	1853	1857	1859	1861	1864
Married					Elizabeth (B1871)
Died		1937	1869	1905	1927
Children	Born	Born	Born	Born	Born
		Grey E. 1897			Gertrude P. 1899

Census addresses:

1901

Back of Bronygan,
Llanfairfechan
Caernarvonshire
With Dorothy (see 3A)

1 back of
95 Porchester Street

Blue indicates jeweller

75

PHILIP VAUGHTON FAMILY TREE

Father

LUKE (B 1828)

	Betty	Lizzie	Thomas E.
Born	1866	1868	1871
Married			Emily (B 1870)
Died		1940	1944

Children

| Born | Born | Born | Edith H | 1896 | Marries Broadbent 1917 |

Census addresses:

1901   1 back of   6 Waterloo Place off Bridge Street West

95 Porchester Street

(With Frederick 3D)

Blue indicates jeweller

76

PHILIP VAUGHTON FAMILY TREE

Father

EDWARD (B 1832)

	Edward E	Amelia E.	Phillip Gilbert	Vincent V	Leonard H	Ada G
Born	1857	1859	1861	1864	1865	1868
Married	Catherine (B 1858)		Jane E (B.1867)			
Died				1936	1938	

Children		Born		Born
Elsie M.	1883		Ada	1885
Ada B.	1886		Dorothy	1887
Edward	1890			
(Died 1965)				

Census addresses:

1891		26 Richmond Rd Handsworth		32 Claremont Rd (With parents)	32 Claremont Rd (With parents)
1901	1 Booth Street Handsworth	124 Croxted Road Camberwell			54 Hollyhead Rd Handsworth (With Maud Smith B. 1892 & 2 Servants)

Blue indicates jeweller

77

PHILIP VAUGHTON FAMILY TREE

Father   Oliver Howard B 1861)

	Annie Reeves-Smith	Catherine May Gertrude.	Howard George	Aileen	Doris	Grace
Born	28.11.1894	11.12.1896	6.7.1898	23.7.1900	3.7.1902	23.5.1905
Married			Susan Marion Anderton			
Died	3.2.1967	3.2.1967	11.12.1970	23.5.1978	9.5.1978	13.11.1979

Children   Born   Brian
                   John

See details on 'Direct Line' tree

Census addresses:

1901   "Goldthorne", Ascot Road

Blue indicates jeweller

APPENDIX 3.

Lodges Associated with Vaughtons
The following records have been complied as a reference to Lodges to whom
Vaughtons have supplied to.

Abbey Lodge No 3778
Abbots Cross Lodge No 814
Abercorn Lodge No 3778
Acacia Lodge No 1582
Acacia Lodge No VII
Adelaide Lodge No 650
Adherence Lodge No 7208
Aeron Lodge No 7208
Afon Dar No 8829
Ala Lodge No 5043
Albatrolss Lodge No 535
Albert Bridge Lodge No 535
Albert Edward - Prince of Wales No 1428
Albert Edward Lodge No 592
Albert Victor Lodge No 1773
Alcvin Lodge No 6300
Aldridge Lodge
Alfreds Lodge No 59
Alloa Lodge No 69
Almacanter Lodge No 7023
Amity Lodge No 3193
Amity Lodge No 5823
Ampthill Lodge MMM No 1396
Ancient Brazen Lodge No 17
Anthea Lodge No 132
Antrim Lodge
Archimede Lodge No 3802
Armagh Home Guard No 747
Arron Lodge No 2240
Arter Lodge No 2654
Arthur Stanley Lodge No 3732
Arthur Sullivan Lodge No 2156
Ashburton Lodge No 2189
Ashford Lodge No 8945
Asley Lodge No 6525
Aston Manor Lodge No 6323
Atholo Lodge No 1004
Balconie Lodge No 764
Ballinory Lodge No 1183
Barry Lodge No 2357
Baswell St James Lodge No 1011
Beacon Lodge No 7915
Bearsden Lodge No 1572
Beaudesert Lodge of MMM No 1350
Bedfordshire Centenary Lodge No 9151
Belfast City Temperance Lodge No 481
Berwick St George Lodge No 4125
Bewick Lodge No 5988
Bewik Lodge No 5988
Birmingham Old Edwardian Lodge No 71
Biscot Lodge No 8801
Bishopbriggs Ldodge No 1259
Bladon Lodge No 839
Blakesley Lodge No 7706

Craigends Lodge No1042
Crawfordsburn Greenock No1121
Crawfordsburn Lodge No 812
Croesco Lodge No 8377
Crumpsall Lodge No 6881
Crusader Lodge No 6589
Crystal Lodge No 4562
Culmore Lodge No 320
Cumberland Kilwinning No 219
Cytringer Lodge No 4048
Dalhouse Bonny Rigg Lodge No 720
Dalry Blair Lodge No 290
Daneswood Lodge No 9087
Dartmoor Lodge No 5604
Daylight Lodge of Hutton
De Bohum Lodge No 8175
De Montfort Lodge No 5155
De Warren Lodge No 1302
Denehead Lodge No 7594
Dinas Llandaf No 8512
Dinas Powis Lodge No 5997
Dolphin Lodge
Donard Lodge No 377
Donnard Lodge No 377
Doric Kilwinning Lodge No 68
Douglas Lodge No 1557
Dover Castle No 7202
Dudley Castle Lodge No 4437
Dumbarton Kilwinning No 18
Dumfries Kilwinnin No 53
Dunham Lodge No 4067
Dunleath Lodge No 654
Duo Fraternitatus Lodge No 9146
Easterhouse Lodge No 1591
Eastern Scotia Lodge No 923sc
Eastmuir Lodge No 1126
Edinburgh St Andrew No 48
Elizabethan Lodge No 100
Elizabethan Lodge No 7341
Elstree & Radlett Mark Lodge No 1315
Emmbrook Lodge No 8786
Endeavour Lodge No 6267
Endeavour Lodge No 829
Endurance Lodge No 5998
Endurance Lodge No 6729
Ernehale Lodge No 8806
Eros Lodge No 801
Eskdale Kilwinning Lodge
Ewenny Lodge No 8405
Excalibur Lodge No 825
Facula Lodge No 4825
Fairham Lodge No 8614
Faithful Lodge
Falls Lodge No 226

Farmers Lodge of Friendship No 9978
Felicity Lodge No 4166
Fellowship Lodge No 6707
Fidelity Lodge No 4902
Fidelity Lodge No 6112
Filton Lodge of Fortitude No 6498
Finchale Priory Lodge
First Lodge of Light No 468
Firth of Clyde Gourock No 626
Forbes Lodge No
Forest of Arden Lodge
Fort William Lodge No 43
Forward Lodge No 1180
Franchelie St Leonard No 6788
Frankley Beeches Lodge No 5846
Fraternith Lodge No 4032
Friendship & Justice Lodge No 5830
Friendship Lodge No 5909
Friendship Lodge No 6169
Gaddesden Lodge NO 3398
Gaen Lodge No 437
Galen Lodge No 6366
Garthland St Winnoch No 205
Gateway Lodge No 8372
Gelligaer Lodge No 6298
Georgetown Lodge No 1170
Gibson Lodge No 87
Gilliland Lodge No 824
Glanfaba Lodge No 2164
Glasgow Kilwinning Lodge
Glasgow Lodge No 441
Glasgow Star Lodge No 219
Glen Council Lodge No 52
Goldieslie Lodge No 9174
Goundale Lodge No 437
Grace Lodge No 8566
Grants Lodge No 8825
Gratitude Lodge No 6514
Green hill Lodge No 6260
Grenock St John No 175
Greyfriars No 1221
Guy's Lodge 395
Gwent Lodge No 8762
Haddenham Lodge No 8944
Hala Lodge No 222
Halcyon Lodge No 5300
Hall Barn Lodge No 8480
Hallamshire Lodgel No 2268
Hampden Lodge No 6483
Han Yang Lodge No 1048sc
Harmonie Lodge No 282
Harmony Lodge No 8414
Harp & Crown Lodge No 60
Harrow St Paul Lodge No 8937

Hartington Lodge No 1085
Hatherton Lodge No 2474
Helenic Lodge No 7270
Helen's Bay Lodge No 934
Henllys Lodge No 8283
Henry Pendrill Charles Lodge No 3769
Highlands Lodge No 1439
Hills Gillhall No 372
Hogganfield Lodge No 1946
Holte Lodge No 1946
Holywell Lodge No 6341
Howardian Lodge No 5317
Hughenden Lodge No 6308
Ibrox Lodge No 1272
Icknield Lodge of MMM No 16250
Impartiality Lodge No 5101
Industria Cambrensis Lodge
Industry Lodge No 240
Integrity Lodge No 989
Irvine St Andrew No 149
Ithon Lodge No 3320
J P M Thmpson Lodge No 349
James Watt Lodge No 5546
Jersey Lodge of Unity No 8352
John Arnott Taylor Lodge No 311
John B Crozier Lodge No 497
Jubilee Lodge No 865
Kendelshire Lodge No 8394
Kenmuir Springburn Lodge No 570
Kennig Lodge No 8289
Kibor Lodge No 4364
Kilwaughter Lodge No 762
King Oswald Lodge No 3306
King William Lodge No 3883
Kings Norton Lodge No 4001
Kings Wston Lodge No 6338
Kingsmere Lodge No 632
Kirkhill Lodge No 1230
Kirkton Hall Lodge No 1614
Knightswood Glasgow Lodge No 1445
Knowle Lodge No 800
Koorosh Lodge No 1574
Kylsyth Lodge No 39
Lancing Lodge No 6352
Lawnbank Lodge No 618
Lee Torre Lodge No 7253
Leslie J Thompson Lodge No 61
Liddell Memorial Lodge No 635
Liscoole Lodge No 763
Livingstone Lodge No 599
Livingstone St Andrews Lodge No 573
Llangattock Lodge No 2547
Lodge Aberethy Round Tower No 1429
Lodge Bannockburn

Lodge Caer Urfa No 4345
Lodge Ce;tic No 291
Lodge Delco No 1624
Lodge Gleniffee Lodge no 1219
Lodge Gordon No 589
Lodge Houston St Johns No 242
Lodge of Ancient Sirling NO 30
Lodge of Anima No 1223
Lodge of Antiquity No 148
Lodge of Benevolence
Lodge of Credence No 7155
Lodge of Devlopment No 6566
Lodge of Dunbar Castle No 75
Lodge of Enterprise No6757
Lodge of Faith No 344
Lodge of Fellowship No 5579
Lodge of Fellowship No 6707
Lodge of Fellowship No 9123
Lodge of Grace No 6211
Lodge of Israel No 1474
Lodge of Journeyman No 8
Lodge of Justice No 65
Lodge of Loch Lomond No 1483
Lodge of Luce Abbey No 689
Lodge of Menorca No 60
Lodge of Orleans No 7955
Lodge of Polkememet No 927
Lodge of Prudence No 2069
Lodge of Seven Hills No 6857
Lodge of St Andrew in the Far East No 4
Lodge of St George No 200
Lodge of St Vincent No 7377
Lodge of the Perfect Ashlar No 8319
Lodge of Unity No 1242
Lodge Pollock No 772
Lodge Possill Park Glasgow No 1330
Lodge Solway No 353
Lodge Southern Cross No 1243
Lodge St Andrew Annan
Lodge St Christopher No 1453
Lodge St John No 189
Lodge Tormohun No 6449
Longridge Lodge No 8077
Lord Arther Lodge No 147
Lord Raglan Lodge No 3685
Lotharna Lodge No 375
Love, Honour & Justice Lodge No 774
Loyal Camrian Lodge No 110
Loyalty Lodge No 4340
Loyalty Lodge No 4819
Loyalty Lodge No 897
Lumley Lodge No 5807
Lyde Lodge No 408
Lyegrove Lodge No 7890

M Creed Meredith Lodge No 253
Machen Lodge No 699
Madragal Lodge No 5039
Maeides Stana Lodge No 7868
Magna Carta No 8017
Major Ness Lodge No 948
Malone Volunteer Lodge
Manchester Engineers Lodge No 4082
Maney Lodge No 7630
Manin Lodge
Mannin Lodge No 7091
Marlborough Lodge No 5335
Marlow Bridge Lodge No 8616
Martlello Lodge No 872
Mauldslie Lodge No 1199
Mawdach Lodge No 1988
Menturia Lodge No 6023
Mercia Lodge No 6246
Mercury Lodge No 7289
Meredith Lodge No 253
Midland Lodge
Military Lodge Jubilee No 2195
Milncroft Lodge No 1515
Milton Lodge No 1520
Minerva Lodge No 1942
Minerval Lodge No 300
Montgomerie Kilwinning Lodge No 624
Moorpark Refrew Lodge No 1263
Mor Hafren Lodge No 7194
Mornington Lodge No 1672
Mosaic Lodge No 5028
Moseley Lodge NO 5224
Mother Kilwinning Lodge
Motherwell Caledonian Lodge No 1228
Mount Aureol Lodge
Mount Edgecumbe Lode No 1544
Mount Lodge No 358
Mount Zion Lodge No 713
Murdos Toun Castle Lodge No 1096
Mystic Quest Lodge
Narbeth Lodge No 2001
Naval & Military Lodge No 40
Naval & Military Lodge No 848
Neath Lodge
Neptune Lodge No 419
New Ilver Jubilee Lodge No 8823
New Monkland Montrose Lodge No 88
Newark Priory Lodge No 5396
Newton Lodge No 8261
Nisbet Iranian Lodge No 1112
Niscot Mark Lodge No 1406
Nitshill Lodge No 1478
North Worcester Lodge No 8180
Northampton Castle MMM No 1346

Nottage Lodge No 8452
Oak Lodge No 877
Oaks of Arden Lodge No 7601
Oban Commercial Lodge No 180
Offa Lodge No 157
Old Albanian Lodge No 4999
Old Carolian Lodge No 7599
Old Dudlian Lodge No 6734
Old Hailey Birian Lodge
Old Halyburian Lodge No 3912
Old Mawoodian Lodge No 7636
Old Monkland St James No 177
Old Plymouthian & Mannmeadian Lodge
Oldham Lodge No 6428
Oncchan Lodge No 6512
Onchan Lodge
Operative Lodge No 203
Operative LODGE No 8783
Orio Lodge No 56
Ormeon Lodge No 499
Ostua Lodge No 1528
Otterspool Lodge No 6605
Paiisley St Mirren
Palantine Lodge No 114
Panmure Lodge No 299
Parkfield Lodge No 5274
Partick St Mary Lodge No 17
Pax Vera Lodge No 6200
Pegasus Lodge
PenHellaz Lodge No 7680
Penlan Lodge No 6695
Perception Lodge No 5424
Perception Lodge No 8492
Perseverance Lodge No 4622
Petitor Lodge No 6857
Pettitor Lodge No 8234
Peveril Lodge No 323
Pidkwic Lodge No 5448
Pollockshaws Royal Arch Lodge No 153
Polynesia Lodge No 562
Pomfret Lodge No 380
Possilpark Lodge No 1330
Power Lodge No 8051
Praewood Lodge No 8919
Press Lodge No 432
Preswynlfa Lodge No 5792
Prince Alfred Lodge No 1218
Prince Arthur Lodge No 4508
Prince of Wales Lodge No 1098
Prince of Wales Lodge No 426
Priory Lodge No 5545
Prospice Lodge No 6663
Quarere Verum Lodge No 914
Queen Victoria Lodfg No 324

Queen Victoriia Lodge No294
Radio Millenium Lodge
Randolph Clarkson Lodge
Ravenhill Lodge No 471
Red Sea Lodge No 919
Regal Lodge NO 6231
Remembrance Lodge No 8323
Rhondda Lodge No 3979
Rickmansworth Lodge No 2218
Riddrie Glasgow Lodge No 1340
Robert Burns Lodge No 440
Robert King Stewart Lodge No 919
Robert Mummery Lodge
Rockingham Forest No 9491
Rokeby Lodge No 6301
Roll Call Lodge No 252
Rosslyn St Clare Lodge
Rother Valley Lodge No 8216
Royal Blues Lodge No 399
Royal Edward Lodge No 892
Royal Orange Lodge No 162
Rushen Lodge N 3944
Ryburn Lodge
Ryton Lodge No 8988
Sandwell Lodge No 4673
Sandwood Glasgow Lodge
Sandye Lodge No 8820
Sapphire Lodge No 5290
Saturnian Lodge No 563l
Scarbo Lodge No 714
Scotia Lodge No 1008
Seafroth Lodge No 854
Septtem Lodge No 7788
Servator Lodge No 6115
Service Lodge No 7139
Seymore LodgeNo 2804
Shaw's Bridge Lodge No 570
Shenstone Lodge No 870
Shenstone Lodge No 7037
Shettleston St John No 128
Shipcote Lodge No 3626
Shir Gar Lodge No 7339
Sibelius Lodge No 9448
Sidon Lodge No 275
Sincerity Lodge No 3850
Sir Francis Drake Lodge No 649
Sir William Wallace Lodge No 1504
Snargate Lodge No 6770
Solihull Lodge No 8088
Solomons Band Lodge No 565
Somers Iles Lodge No 1503
South Kent Lodge No 4303
South Western No 1242
Spencer Walpole Temperance Lodge N

Sphere Lodge No 5051
Spiers id Elderslie
Spithead Lodge No 6719
St Amry Lodge No 3879
St Andrew Cumbernauld Lodge No 119
St Andrew Lochlee Lodge
St Andrew Lodge No 215
St Andrew Lodge No 2541
St Andrew Lodge No 465
St Andrew Lodge No 469
St Andrew Lodge No 524
St Andrew Lodge No 601
St Andrew Lodge No 803
St Andrews Lodge No 25
St Augustines Lodge No 9018
St Barchan Lodge No 156
St Barnabas Lodge No 5050
St Bartholomew Lodge No 6378
St Bartholomew Lodge No 696
St Bernard Lodge of Research
St Blaise Lodge No6113
St Christopher Lodge No 5999
St Christopher Lodge No 6796
St Clair Lodge Edinburgh
St Clair Lodge No 362
St Clair Lodge No 427
St Clement Lodge No 1353
St Clement Lodge No 202
St Columba Lodge No 637
St Columba Lodge No 729
St Columba Temperance Lodge
St David Lodge No 76
St Deny Lodge No 8250
St Donards Lodge No 676
St Edmunds Lodge No 7377
St Enoch Lodge No 1288
St Euny Lodge No 6025
St George Carrickfergus Lodge No 1016
St George Lodge No 431
St George Lodge No 5691
St Giles Lodge No 8555
St Giles Lodge Oxford No 8904
St Gwynno Lodge No 8599
St Helens Ldge No 641
St Ilan Lodge No 6624
St Illtyd Mark Lodge No 784
St James Harthill Lodge
St James Lodge No 1116
St James Lodge No 125
St James Lodge No 590
St John Busby No 458
St John Dalmuir No 543
St John Dalziel No 406
St John Kilwinning Largs No 173

St John Lodge No 11
St John Lodge No 162
St John Lodge No 252
St John Lodge No 406
St John Lodge No 6320
St John Lodge No 68
St John Midcalder No 272
St John Slamannan No 484
St John Whiteinch No 683
St John's Campbeltown No 141
St John's Lodge No 6414
St Judes Lodge NO XXVI
St Kenelm Lodge No 6082
St Kenneth Lodge No 1441
St Keran No 1155
St Margarets Lodge No 7349
St Mark Lodge No 6969
St Mark Lodge No 8479
St Martin Lodge No 7986
St Martins Porchway Lodge No 4862
St Mary Lodge No 30
St Mary Lodge No 5148
St Matthew Lodge No 549
St Medans Lodge No 1335
St Nicholas Lodge No 1014
St Pancras Lodge
St Paul's Lodge No 43
St Pauls Lodge No 6516
St Peters Lodge No 476
St Piranis Lodge No 7620
St Queninis Lodgwe No 306
St Servanus Lodge No 771
St Thomas Lodge No 306
St Trinians Lodge No 2050
Staple Hill Lodge No 6043
Star of Ards Lodge No 183
Star of Bethlehem Lodge No 665
Star of Down Lodge No 435
Steadfasr Lodge No 5960
Stechford Lodge No3185
Stormont Masonic Lodge No 560
Stranmillis Lodge No 568
Streatham Hill Lodge No 3784
Streetly Lodge No 7488
Studley Lodge
Summit Lodge No 5944
Sun Lodge No 638
Sutton Pilgrims Lodge No 7780
Talygarn Lodge
Tarbolton Kilwinning St James No 135
Taverners Lodge
Teddington St Mary Lodge No 7469
Temperance Lodge
Temple Lodge No 4929

Temple Lodge No 5881

Temple of Ards No 739

Templemore Temperance Lodge No 306

The Mount Lodge No 358

Thistle & Crown Lodge No 1167

Thistle & Rose Lodge No 169

Thistle & Rose Lodge No 6644

Thistle & Rose Lodge of Bedfordshire No

Thistle Lodge No 1014

Thistle Lodge No 62

Thomas Telford Lodge No 2029

Thorntree Lodge No 512

Three Shires Lodge No 5103

Three Spires Lodge No 6940

Three Spires Lodge No 9245

Tollcross Lodge

Trafalgar Lodge No 971

Trafalgar Lodgel No 4668

Trevaunance Lodge No 4668

Tring Lodge No 5001

Trinity Lodge No 8586

Tudor Rose Lodge No 5660

Tynwald Lodge No 1242

Umvuma Lodge No 1157

Union & Crown Lodge No 407

Union Band Lodge No 35

Unitas Fratrum Lodg No 788

Unity Larne Lodge No 706

Unity Lodge No 1510sc

Unity Lodge No 383

Unity Lodge No 7026

Upper Tahmes Lodge No 8696

Vale Lodge No 6632

Vale of Castiard Lodge No 7186

Veneration Lodge No 5686

Victory Lodge No 8506

Vigilant Lodge No 456

Viking Lodge NO 6335

Viking Lodge NO 6335

Vivian Lodge No 8267

Wallacwe Lodge No 146

Walmley St John No 6504

Wandsworth Lodge No 802

Wellingon Lodge No 1385

Wellington Lodge No 82

Wemyss Lodgfe No 777

West Buckland School Lodge No 90377

Western Tideways Lodge No 8119

Wheatfield Lodge No 582

White Horse Lodge No 2227

White Roase LodgeNo 6781

White Rose Lodge No 6781

Whitehall Lodge No 520

William of Colchester Lodge

Willowbank Lodge No 7439

Wodlands Lodge No 4447

Woodhall St John Lodge

Woodhall St John No 305

Woodvale Lodge No 572

Worcester Lodge No 280

Wycombe Lodge No 1501

Wythall Lodge No 5665

Y Bont Faen Lodge

Ymlaen Lodge No NO 8419

Ystrad Mynach Lodge No 8567

Zetland Lodge No 391

THE AUTHOR

TIM GROWCOTT

Since 1992 Tim Growcott has been the Senior Partner in Halcyon Environmental, a UK based consultancy, which specialises in Environmental Consulting Services.

Trained formally as an Industrial Chemist, he has worked with companies including Mander Brothers (Wolverhampton) in paints, BL Heavy Vehicles Division at Guy Motors in heavy vehicle manufacturing and Wilkins & Mitchell (Wednesbury) in domestic appliance manufacturing.

He worked with the Inmont Corporation and BASF in automotive and printing industry coatings development, producing paints for Ford, British Leyland, Vauxhall and Rolls Royce, and then SGS in specialist environmental roles, undertaking diverse environmental issues including sales, marketing, site investigation work, litigation and liability, the development of environmental systems including EN ISO 14001.

Tim has produced short histories for companies including Bayliss, Jones and Bayliss (producers of railings and railway components to the world), and Hingley's who produced boilers in Cradley Heath and notably some of the anchors for RMS Titanic.

Tim provided support to W H Darby in support of their bid for the Olympic medal whence this volume was first considered.

Currently he is working on additional historical short books for Tavira in Portugal and the famed knights of the siege of 1242 and a never ending fiction based on his involvement in the investigation of international perfume frauds in the early 1990s.

ACKNOWLEDGEMENTS

This work could not have been completed without the support of:

Jan Growcott for her proofing, archiving assistance, layout work and arrangements.

Steve and Dani Hobbis and the entire workforce of W H Darby who provided many of the items photographed and archived at the Well Street and Livery Street premises.

Dr Sally Bagot of the Birmingham Assay Office.

Corinna Raynor, Senior Archivist - Collections Department, of the Archives and Heritage Department of Birmingham Central Library for access to their collections.

Tony Abrahams, Midlands Historical data, who assisted in procuring the Directory information.

Barbara Riley who catalogued many of the exemplary work pieces provided by W H Darby.

Diane Clements, Director at the Library and Museum of Freemasonry, Freemason's Hall, London.

Sarah Latham of Halcyon who "set the page" and collated the PowerPoint work and who stamped her style on the presentations and layouts.

Clint and Kathrin at Hatters (formerly Gothic Works), for their assistance in availing the photographs taken at their hostel.

Finally our heartfelt thanks go to John and Brian Vaughton, now living in Monmouth and Exminster respectively, who so freely gave of their anecdotes and memorabilia.

"Finally I have to thank my wife Jan, my two sons, Ross and Richard, my daughter Charlotte and all of our friends who supported me in getting this all together.

I promise not ever to do it again until the next time..."